Seventh Son of an Irishman

DON MAHONEY

Copyright © 2024 Don Mahoney
All rights reserved
First Edition

PAGE PUBLISHING
Conneaut Lake, PA

First originally published by Page Publishing 2024

ISBN 979-8-89157-274-4 (pbk)
ISBN 979-8-89157-284-3 (digital)

Printed in the United States of America

A memoir for my family and friends, including those who helped me enjoy life excitingly, especially my wife, Donna.

I was born the seventh son of eight siblings. This story is based on true events as I remember them. My mother was Doris Courtney, and my father was John Mahoney. They married and had eight children, seven boys and one girl. Each one has interesting life stories, but growing up together kept us all very close and was an adventure every day.

Doris was a saint, raising all those children, running a household, and making sure we were all fed, clean, and dressed every day. She was born in 1918 in the same hospital that we were all born in and attended the same high school we all attended, where she was valedictorian. She really could do anything and everything but early in her life decided to get married and raise a family.

John (Jack) worked at various jobs growing up, always tough hard labor. He was a tall (six feet and five inches) strapping man, and I remember these huge hands that were as leathery and large as a baseball glove. He was also considered handsome as I found out later in life that the neighborhood women would peer out and watch him while he was loading up his truck to prepare for the day's work. I had a good laugh over that revelation.

He was tough; they called him Jackson PDQ (pretty damn quick) due to his hot temper and fast hands, a trait I inherited through my teenage years. Don't get me wrong; he wasn't mean, but he would never back down and was fearless. He had a brother, Harry, who had two sons, and also had a sister, Edna. She had a daughter, Donna, my favorite cousin with a wonderful laugh. I'll tell you a little about Donna later.

Doris did work before children but decided early in her life she would rather be a mother and housewife. Yes, those terms were acceptable unlike the current opinion of some people in current times that might not like being referred to by actual pronouns. Doris was the only girl of six children. Her brothers, my uncles, were all fighting WW2 veterans: Uncle Jack, Vinnie, Donald (my namesake), Kenny, and Billy. A lot of them saw action. I remember stories about them, especially Billy, who was wounded and became a prisoner of war. None of those veterans of the greatest generation liked to talk about war, much like veterans of Vietnam who do not like to talk about their experiences either, but I remember Uncle Bill showing me his wounds in his torso that you could stick your finger into the bullet holes (I actually remember doing that as a child). That impacted me and made me think I would never want to go to war.

Doris was funny and talented, the life of the party with her musical talent of playing the piano. She did not read music, but if she heard it, she in seconds could play it. She played by ear, usually upbeat honky-tonk, but could pretty much play anything on an old stand-up piano. She sometimes would play while she was alone, but if there was an event or party, we would always encourage her to play to get the party started.

My father, Jack, went into the navy but was discharged early for some medical reason. I think it had to do with a breathing issue he had. He did work at one time in a paint factory, and I remember a story about him losing his temper at someone saying something I'm sure was probably a comment about my mother.

The story goes: He held the guy over a vat of boiling paint, and the guy's hat fell off and disintegrated (poof) just above the vat. He apparently got fired over that, thus the nickname PDQ. He was a laborer all his life and worked hard and partied harder. He could work hard all day, but at the end of work was happy hour, where he could unwind at the local gin mill. He could most likely be found at his favorite hangout, the Southside Hotel owned by Arty Schiller, and everyone called the place Schillers. It was a bar and grill with an old-style ornate bar with a number of tables in a back room for eating, but the draw was the bar. The old man would sometimes take one of us with him and give us a soda but wouldn't let us sit at the bar unless it was a special occasion. Schillers was part of our education, watching men interact playing cards and dice and betting on horse races and ballgames, all part of growing up in a working-class town of laborers, baymen, and fishermen.

Schillers would be the hangout for generations of locals and was always the choice to see friends. It would sometimes get rough with the drinking, gambling, and someone losing, so you had to keep on your toes, but boy it was fun.

Jackson PDQ liked gambling, and one of his favorite pastimes was playing a card game that was made popular in the navy called cribbage. It wasn't always luck, but there was some skill involved, and he was a good player. Usually, the loser buys. He loved horse racing too, and one of his close friends, Jim McCulley, wrote for *The Daily News* sports section on racing news, and Jack would go to the track with him from time to time. One of my early memories is going to the racetrack and sitting in the press box with all the writers smoking their cigars and drinking something I'm pretty sure wasn't soft drinks. Jackson won some and lost some, but he knew he had responsibilities at home and never really got carried away—that I remember. I will relate a story about his gambling later on as I got older and how I confronted a bookie (yes, there really are bookies especially back in those days). There would be loud raucous crowds at Schillers. I remember an urn stored above the bar with what I think was the original owner with a tie wrapped around it. It was done out of respect because apparently everyone liked him.

Once in a while, my father would take one of us to work with him, I think to prepare us for our future. When I went with him as a young man, he was working as a billposter. That was someone who put the signs on advertising billboards, which were plentiful in those days and a major form of advertising. Man, that was tough work all seasons—hot in summer, cold in winter, and not for the weak at heart. It took strength, agility, and actual bravery to carry and climb the ladders, scrape off the old signs, and paste up the new signs. You could not have a fear of heights and do that job. He taught me to be fearless. It really took talent to do what he did, and he was pretty much a legend in the industry. Everyone called him Bridge Route because part of his territory was the bridges in New York billboards, where he had to climb and hang over bridges to put up signs—very dangerous. In the winter months, the paste was mixed with water and could easily freeze, so he would have to mix it just before he went up the ladder using his bare hands to brush it on and open the paper bills with his fingers, no gloves. That made his hands even tougher.

Jack made us laugh many times with his dry sense of humor, sayings like what he would call people. One he would use all the time with someone he didn't care for was *meathead*: "What a meathead!" He used this term way before anyone else, including Archie Bunker who was in a TV show called *All in the Family*. We always thought they stole that line from my father because he would use that line way before that TV show was even on. Another term he used all the time was *porch-climbing crook*. He used that for everyone, whether or not he liked them. Another derogatory name was *chowder head*, usually referring to New Englanders, primarily Massachusetts. He didn't care for anyone not from New York, especially if they rooted for another pro team.

We lived in what was originally a small three-bedroom summer cottage, a few houses from the Great South Bay, with no air conditioning, and the only heat was an oil-fired heater designed with a fan standing right on the floor at the top of the small dining room meant to heat the small kitchen behind it and the three small bedrooms along the right and straight into the living room at the front of the house. The design of the house was functional, with a back door exiting from the kitchen and a porch at the front with a front door to a tiny front yard. The front yard was played on so much, no grass would have a chance to grow. We had to use the back door to enter the house if you wanted to avoid the wrath of PDQ! The front door was what is known as French doors with multiple panes of glass. PDQ spent time replacing glass after one of us would throw a ball or rock and break one of the panes. One day, he was replacing one of them while we were all playing in our little front yard, and one of us broke another pane while he was in the middle of replacing it. He just stood up staring at the door for a second and proceeded to break all the panes out of the door, turned around, and said, "Now you can't break anymore!" We froze for a second and then scattered.

"Run for the hills!" Doris made him fix them, saying, "They were just being boys," and he eventually forgave us. We never broke another window again.

The layout explanation has some importance to some of the stories that took place at that house. The winters could be brutal when we would all have to get up early to get ready for school, and the battles began for positioning in front of the heater to warm up before the next battle for the one bathroom at the back of the house with a toilet and a bathtub. Sometimes, the battle would get out of hand until you heard Doris holler, "Jack!" My father would feign, removing his belt to whack us, and he would make sure everyone cooled down. When he started to take off his belt, we would scatter and run for the hills.

The next battle would be getting dressed for school and having to walk two miles to Saint Patrick's parochial school in all kinds of weather—heat, rain, snow, or wind. Long Island is known for unpredictable weather. It didn't matter; we had to be in school on time. Oh, by the way, Doris made sure Saturday night was bath night so we would be nice and clean for Sunday mass and school the rest of the week. Yes, one bath per week, unless there was a special occasion. I wouldn't change my childhood for anything. Some things changed as I matured, but it was an adventure every day.

Mom made sure we brushed our teeth, washed up with a washcloth, and put on clean clothes every day. If we were to go to school, we had to wear uniforms that made it easy to choose what to wear. Uniforms had to be purchased, and I know that was a strain on our parent's budget, as not much money was available, but my mother scrimped and saved just so we could get what she thought was a good education. Other than the uniforms, the kids' clothes were primarily hand-me-downs, which didn't always fit exact but were clean. I would joke about by the time I got shoe hand-me-downs, the only thing left were the laces. It wasn't always easy, but Mahoneys were very good at adapting.

There was another place Jack would like to hang out. It was a bar around the corner of our house named Vinnie's Happy Landing. I think they named it that because it was near a boat landing because it wasn't such a happy landing when they threw your ass out!

The owner was friends with our family for decades, Vinnie Abbottacola, an American Italian whom everyone called Vinnie Abbott because they couldn't pronounce his last name. There were more gambling, cribbage card games, dice, a pool table, and an old-style bar room. Again, sit at a table and have a soda if you happened to be with my dad. Sports was on TV all the time, horse races, baseball, and football. Football was split between Giant Fans and Jet Fans and baseball with either Mets or Yankees fans. Don't ever root for an opposing city team, or you would have a happy landing. Everybody in there were tough guys, fishermen, or construction workers, all kinds of laborers, but once in a while, there would also be a white-collar banker or a Wall Street type, and they would all enjoy being there. Bay Shore's population was a mix of poor, middle class, and very wealthy Manhattan commuters.

Bay Shore train station was an hour ride to New York City.

Our home was the gathering place for family and friends for parties on holidays. This small little bungalow would then be packed with music, laughter, adult family and friends, and us kids and our friends. Everyone would bring a dish, so there would always be plenty of food during the holidays. Speaking of food, there was a time when PDQ had had enough of us. "You kids are eating me out of house and home!" He put a chain with a lock around the refrigerator. Doris made him take it off, but it did make a point.

Jackson PDQ was originally a Brooklyn Dodgers fan but, like most New Yorkers, disowned them when they left for the West Coast. "Those traitors," he would say. He would sit in his easy chair near the front door, watching games, and complain about the teams when they weren't playing well, which was pretty constant in the early days of the New York Mets. We all followed his lead, rooting for New York teams. Some of us were Mets and Jets fans, some Yankees and Giant fans. I was a Jets fan! Jackson PDQ complained about Namath's long hair but would still root for the Jets, especially if they were playing the Patriots. He would make comments like "get that porch-climbing crook." Sometimes, more entertaining to listen to him than the actual announcers.

I did confront a bookie that was taking bets from PDQ when I witnessed him upsetting my father over a bet he made and the guy refusing to pay him. I told this guy if he took another bet from my father, he would have to deal with me, and I was serious! That didn't stop PDQ from gambling, but just not with that particular bookie.

Number 1 Son

I want to start with the firstborn and continue with the rest of my siblings and each of their stories.

John Vincent was named after our father. We refer to him as Jay or Jason as I call him (everyone has nicknames in our family). He was and still is one of the smartest men I know, and I still ask him for answers and advice for a variety of different things. I know he is humble about how bright he is and wouldn't like that I tell people how smart but tough he is. I'm writing this and can say what I want.

We all grew up in a little three-bedroom cottage on Great South Bay, and when it started to get too crowded and he was starting a career, he temporarily moved in with my mother's mother, Cecilia "Celi" Courtney, who lived a few houses away.

Jay eventually moved into the city and shared a flat with one of our cousins for a short time. I remember visiting there once when I was a kid, and even though we grew up in a tiny house, I thought it had a very small kitchen, bedroom, small living space, and a tiny bathroom. For some reason, I think Jay slept on a sofa in what was generously called a living room.

He started his successful career commuting, where he met his wife, Donna. Donna was originally from Queens, and boy did she have a tough New York upbringing and attitude. Jay was more reserved, and they are a perfect match. They met when Jay was working in Manhattan as a retail manager, and she was his secretary (assistant was not the term in those days). She tells the story about how she chased him around the desk and finally caught him. She has a great sense of humor that she and her husband passed on to their children.

Their children prove what good parents they were as they all grew up to be good people whom we are very close to. John Vincent III (Jayvee), Darrin, (Darwin), Lisa (Beesa), and Tara (Mara or princess-lol) are great kids. Jayvee went on to become a grammar school principal with children of his own. I'm very close to Darrin's family and will talk about him later. Lisa is a wild, very talented, lovable girl and the best athlete, while Tara is a sweetheart, very beautiful, and married to Jim, an outdoorsman, with twin boys who are also outdoorsmen (hunters, campers, surfers).

I am close to my brother Jay and, as I said, very close to Darrin and his family. One reason we are so close is, they plan a vacation every year to visit us and we have so much fun with them. Michele is a saint and a great cook along with their beautiful daughter Taylor. We always eat too much when they are in town! Madison and Devon are both beautiful too and have Darrin's sense of humor and keep us laughing the whole time we are together. Danny, the only boy, is one of those kids who were probably born in the wrong era. He would fit right into the sixties. The whole family is very talented.

Jay (Jason) started his own retail operation that grew into a number of outlets, and his children all chipped in to help the business grow. After years of success, they finally started their own successful careers and families and moved a number of times, starting in Long Island in Islip, close to Bayshore, Michigan, and now, most of them live in Pennsylvania, and I think Lisa lives in Virginia.

Jay (Jason) is now in his eighties and still working, having gotten into insurance later in his life to keep busy, still successful and sharp as a tack. His cognition is very much intact, not like some of the current so-called leaders who are supposedly running our country now.

He really is a good guy, and I love him and his entire family. We would sometimes meet in the city, the two Donnas, me, and Jay, and always had fun and sometimes would get into trouble, barhopping or going to various restaurants. Jay always knew the good restaurants for good food and would be happy if the service was good but would definitely let them know if it wasn't!

We all played sports in high school, and Jay played football for Bay Shore. He was a center, and if you ask anyone who played the sport, center was always considered the smartest line position. That was Jay.

Second Son

Patrick "Pat/Fatrack" Mahoney is the second son. Pat was one of the most athletic Mahoneys (we were all pretty good athletes). He played all sports at Bay Shore High School, excelling in football, basketball, swimming, and diving. He played football as a quarterback and was captain of both football and basketball. He was considered short for a Mahoney but was fast, had a rocket arm, and could shoot baskets from anywhere on the court. He was a good swimmer and became a lifeguard as a young man. We grew up next to a town beach called Benjamin's Beach we called Benji's. The beach had boardwalks going out and around into the bay and had diving boards including high boards and platforms, which Patrick got really accomplished at using. He was graceful and athletic, and I swear he and my brother Terry could have been Olympic divers; they were that good.

As he got a little older, he got married to Maureen and started a family. They had three children, Tracy, Courtney, and Patrick Junior. Tracy went to school on a music scholarship for her operatic voice that is beautiful. Everyone would ask her to sing at events, weddings, etc., which I'm sure got old to her, so she went back to law school and became an attorney. She also married an attorney and started her own family. Courtney went on to follow her sister to law school and also received a degree and, believe it or not, married another attorney and started a family. Patrick Junior is working and living on Long Island, and he inherited his father's sense of humor and is very funny.

Pat went on to a career in law enforcement. He joined Suffolk County Police Department. He became a patrolman and began to make his mark in the department through hard work and determination. He eventually became a detective and ended up running the Auto Theft Squad, with many results of catching thieving crooks.

After his success, he started to become political and was elected president of the Detectives Association of Suffolk County Police Department. His career started to ascend from there.

I remember a story that he and his partner were driving down the street near our home, and they spotted a man face down on the sidewalk. It turned out he was waiting for somebody to come to his aid so he could surprise and mug them, something he had done a number of times. When Pat turned him over to check if he was okay, this guy punched him in the face—*big mistake*! Of course, that guy went to jail. I hate to think what happened to him before he was actually imprisoned. Pat had a great sense of humor and was always ready with some wisecrack or joke. I still laugh at some of his old jokes, especially ones that weren't always G-rated.

Patrick served with honor and eventually retired from Suffolk County Police to run for County Legislature and was elected for a couple of terms. After that, he decided to run for sheriff of Suffolk County and was elected.

The sheriff ran the jail in Riverhead with multiple county sheriffs that controlled and transported prisoners among a number of other duties. He was always good at making sure his deputies were respected, and he was well liked by everyone I ever met.

I remember a story about one of our neighbors who grew up with us, whom Pat saw in a jail cell when he was doing an inspection. When Pat saw him, he asked, "What are you doing here?"

Benny, as we called him, replied "Six months!"

We called him Benny the Burglar from then on.

The New York political scene has and always will be cutthroat, and some were crooked. Pat did make some real enemies during his political career, and they attempted to take him down. They tried their best but lost in the end, and those who tried were finally found to be crooked themselves. People in glasshouses shouldn't throw accusations.

Pat eventually retired and moved on to divorce Maureen and married Marilyn. He moved to Vero Beach, Florida. I would visit him from time to time, and he would always make me laugh. He competed with our other brothers to be the funniest but would compete with our brother Mike the most. It was like attending a comedy show when they were together. The two of them were very close in more ways than just humor. We lost Pat just recently to a lung ailment called interstitial lung disease, which he said was caused by getting a covid vaccine (China virus). The fear of being attacked kept doctors from blaming the virus for a variety of problems. It is my opinion that the vaccine caused many more problems for people than the government will ever admit to and also future problems especially for otherwise healthy young people, where, again, in my opinion, you will see all kinds of bad results from getting a covid vaccine. The people who experimented with this virus will someday be held accountable for the many lives they were responsible for taking and in my opinion should be tried for murder. You can come to your own conclusions about who I am talking about.

Third Son

Michael "Moose" Mahoney is son number three. Mike was the heart of the family—a big man, kind of a gentle giant but still with the Mahoney temper when needed. Strong and big, he also played football at Bay Shore High School along with my brother Terry. Mike was a good-enough player to have done something to go on playing from high school sports, but the family financial situation would have made it tough. He played lineman in a couple of games against a player who went on to play in the NFL for Dallas, and Mike kicked his ass.

When he graduated, he ended up in the army during the Vietnam War and was thankfully stationed in Texas. His duty was as a bartender in The Officers Club, where he served off-duty officers who would go to wind down in the club, so much so that often would end up with Mike breaking up fights, and that kept him in good standing with the officers as they knew he would cover for them. "Pretty sweet duty," my other brothers who served would say. I can't remember if he was first or if Pat was, but they both ended up in the Suffolk County Police Department and continued having a successful career.

Many stories of him as a patrolman were pretty comical. Again, he competed with Pat as another comedian in our family. One of the funny stories was a call he went onto at a building called Pilgrim State, an abandoned mental hospital. What happened when he arrived on scene was a disturbed man with a rifle was on the roof of the building, and when Mike exited his patrol car, this guy began to fire at him. Mike told the story about how his big ass scrambled to try and get under his patrol car. They subsequently arrested that idiot. It wasn't just New York City that had idiots; Long Island had some.

Another funny story was about someone he went to school with. George Frayne was his name, and he was a musician later known as Commander Cody of Commander Cody and his Lost Planet Airmen. George would visit our home and play my mother's piano and pretend he was Jerry Lee Lewis, even going so far as kicking the piano stool out from under him just like Jerry Lee would. I remember my mother running through the house screaming, "George, George, stop banging on my piano!"

George went out to the West Coast and had a pretty successful career with hits like "Boy Your Gonna Drive Me to drinking, if You Don't Stop Driving That Hot Rod Lincoln" and "Smoke, Smoke, Smoke that Cigarette."

George came back one year, and Mike got a call of a disturbance. When he started to get close to the call, he realized it was George's mother's house. George had gotten home and was still on West Coast time and had taken his hot rod out and was racing it up and down the street. When Mike arrived, he saw George's tour bus in the driveway, and when he saw George, he said, "George, you can't be racing up and down the street especially this late at night."

George's response was, "Mike, don't call me George in front of the band. Call me Commander!"

Pat was really close to Mike, and they busted each other's balls constantly. Pat would sometimes call him Toody, after a character on a TV show named *Car 54* with Toody and Muldoon, two haphazard cops who were very funny.

Mike was a good cop. All his partners loved him, and the rest of the force respected him enough that they elected him president of the PBA (Patrolmen's Benevolent Association), and they continued to reelect him until his retirement. As president, he was responsible for negotiating contracts for the force and was so accomplished at it that for his term as president, Suffolk County was the highest-paid police department in the country. Our family was very proud of him. Mike married local girl Liz, and they had three kids, Beth, Michael Junior, and Michele—all good kids, typical Mahoneys with the Mahoney sense of humor. Another part of his presidency was protecting cops accused of wrongdoing by making sure they had good representation.

Listen, I knew plenty of cops, and most of them are really good people doing their job to protect and to serve. Just like any large group of people, there are good ones and bad ones. The ones I thought should not be cops were the ones who were pretty much cowards until they got a badge and a gun that inflated their ego—tough guys only when they became cops! A recent example was the Parkland Shooting school resource officer. What a coward! There should not only be better protection for kids in schools, but any resource officer should be screened and required to take an oath to protect children and teachers put in that situation, period. Mike passed away too early after his retirement. He was only fifty-nine.

Mike (Moose) running his boat through Great River

Fourth Son

Terrence "Terrible Terry the Termite" Mahoney, the fourth son, came along right after Mike. (They called us Irish twins because we were all born so close to each other.) Terry and Pat competed for being the best athlete of the family, and I think Terry probably was the winner. He played football at the same time as Mike and was a punishing running back and linebacker. He not only was ferocious on the gridiron but also was a state champion wrestler at the most competitive weight class. Boy was he a good wrestler, but his teammates were all great wrestlers also, and they remained close friends forever. It was exciting to watch him play football and to wrestle. They were such fans of wrestling they would travel the country for years to the NCAA national wrestling competitions no matter what state they might be held. Terry joined the Air Force during the Vietnam War era and was stationed in Spain, fueling jets.

When he returned, he started working at Suffolk County Water Authority. Terry was what people would call a stubborn Irishman, but he made many good longtime friends there. He just never got along with some of the bosses and authority figures and would get in trouble with them from time to time. Once, he got into some trouble, and his boss, as a punishment, forced him to repaint an office. When he arrived at the office and asked his boss what he wanted painted, his boss replied, "Everything." Terry went on to paint everything, including phones, typewriters, and all.

When his boss went crazy, Terry's response was, "You said paint everything." That was the last time he was punished! Terry the Terror would sometimes push my father to the edge, and Jack would respond.

The three bedrooms were the front bedroom, for my mother and father and when Gina was a baby; the middle room for Pat, Mike, and Terry; and the rear bedroom for the rest of us. The bedrooms got juggled around from time to time, but the middle room was where we planned to annoy our parents. I remember my father chasing Terry into the middle room and him diving under the bed. My father tried to reach him, but he would just scurry away. My father picked the bed up and moved it to grab him, and Terry would just crab crawl to the other side. This went on till my father got tired of chasing him. It was pretty comical to watch.

Terry married Patricia and had a daughter, Jackie, who is a sweetheart. Terry, when he was younger, did have the Mahoney temper and showed it quite often. Sometimes, all it took was a few drinks, and he would turn into a terror, whom you really didn't want to be around.

He finally got his temper under control when he quit drinking and is now the most docile nice guy you would ever meet. Terry divorced Pat and married Carol and is the most caring man I have ever met. He would give you the shirt off his back if you needed it and is that dependable.

Fifth Son

Brian "Mooncat" Mahoney showed up after Terry. Another Bay Shore athlete, he played football as an end. Mooncat (his nickname given to him by our brother Mike, the result of his wild nights as a teenager), Terry, Mike, and Brian were very close and had many of the same friends growing up. Yes, he has the Mahoney humor. We all got chased by Jack for bad behavior from time to time, but it seemed like Brian was running or hiding from the old man more than the rest of us. Brian worked with Terry at the Water Authority for a short time, but the first thing he did was join the Marine Corps on the buddy system with a few of his friends. He and his friends made that decision when one night they were teenagers sneaking through the woods of an all-female private school's estate to conduct a panty raid. They actually thought that experience and getting away with it qualified them to be soldiers.

Brian was the only brother out of four who served during Vietnam to see action. There was a story about his deployment leaving from the West Coast on a ship. The marines had been given a leave before leaving for combat. Every marine had made it back to the ship when it was due to disembark, except Mooncat. He had gotten into some trouble in town and ended up getting an escort from the MPs in a Jeep, and when arriving to the dock, everyone in the ship was waiting on the side of the railings, watching him pull up, standing at the back of the Jeep with his hands raised up as if he had just won a championship fight, and the whole crew was cheering him on. He spent a couple of days in the brig on the way to fight.

He was a decorated marine that was in more than his share of firefights. He was what they call a Gunner and had a team that supported him while in combat. A gunner is apparently a prime target of the enemy because of the high destruction and cover protection a gunner provides for the other troops. He was in many battles and received accommodations and medals including a purple heart for being wounded in combat. My father and mother received letters from a few of his fellow marines (they had a different nickname for him, "Jake") and officers explaining his bravery under combat. He was even expected to receive a major medal called The Bronze Star, but upon his discharge, that Irish temper that the Mahoneys are known for got the best of him when his commanding officer pulled rank on him when they had gotten back to the States. This was a guy I was told by other marines who fought with Brian that Brian's action had saved this guy's ass a number of times. I can't say exactly what Brian's response was, but it cost him the award. He could care less, and we all were just happy to have him home safe.

When Mooncat was discharged, he did go to work with Terry at the Water Authority but planned and took the test to become a Suffolk County cop.

He became a cop and served to retirement age on the police force, starting as a patrolman and eventually becoming an investigator for the District Attorney's office. He also did some undercover work and was set up in a fencing operation to stop a ring of thieves. They set him up in a shop and spread the word to these local crooks where they could sell their stolen goods and they didn't know they were being filmed. These idiots weren't really the brightest most of the time, even trying to sell stolen vehicles. Brian had driven one home one night before he had to be back on shift, and while he was trying to rest up, he heard the car start and realized his son had taken the car for a joyride without realizing it was a stolen car. Brian almost had a coronary before he caught up to him to return the car!

Brian had married Helen when he was in the marines and had three children, Brian Junior, Kerri, and Allison. I am close to most of my nephews and nieces, but I am especially close to Kerri for reasons I will explain later.

Sixth Son

Dennis "The Menace" Mahoney is son number six. I was born right after Dennis, and again, we are another pair of Irish twins. Just so you know, we consider ourselves Americans first of Irish descent. I think every American should use the American term first, no matter what country their family originated from or their heritage, for example, American Irish, American Italian, American Black, American German, and so on. We are all Americans.

Dennis attended Saint Patrick's like the rest of the Mahoneys did and then attended Bay Shore High School. Dennis was always well-liked and good at making friends. He was another string of Mahoney athletes playing football but excelled more in wrestling on another great wrestling team. One of his teammates and friends was one of our neighbors, Larry "Murphy" Benson. Murphy was another champion like my brother Terry. I'm pretty sure he never lost a match. Dennis was as wild as any of us in school. He and Murphy got into trouble once on a bus when on the way to another school to wrestle. They had stuck their bare asses out of the bus windows to moon passersby and were caught and busted. Mr. Thieban issued the punishment. They never told me what it was, but I'm pretty sure it was embarrassing.

Another great team to watch—Bay Shore had a reputation for being a top-notch educational school along with great athletic programs in all sports. Dennis did have a little musical talent that Mom tried to cultivate by getting him piano lessons. His teacher's name was Mr. Shapel, who would come to our home to teach Dennis how to play and read music. We all made fun of the teacher because he would wear these extremely wide ties that were not in fashion. We all made fun of him secretly. One day, when we were in the house, a knock came on the front door from the piano teacher. Terry answered the door and told him, "You can't come in now. I'm watching TV!" Mom was not happy. Dennis didn't keep up lessons and stopped playing. I wish he would have continued.

Dennis did have the Mahoney sense of humor and surrounded himself with friends who were funny also. One of his best friends was Ned Baker. Ned was funnier than most anyone else, and we were all together all the time. Ned would crash at our house from time to time, especially if we were out gallivanting. One winter night, we snuck in with Jackson sleeping in his easy chair by the front door. We used to also sneak cigarettes in the house, open the window in the middle bedroom, and blow the smoke out. Ned left the cigarettes in the car and decided to go out the window to get them. He had already undressed to go to bed, and it was snowing out. When he went out, we closed the window and locked it, making it so he would have sneak back in past PDQ in his underwear. He was almost in tears, begging us to let him back in the window, so we did, laughing our asses off at him. I'm sure he got even with us somehow later.

Dennis went to school with his future wife, Linda. Linda was a cheerleader, and when she reads this, she is going to give me a hard time for mentioning that. Dennis had other talents also and was the star of the senior class play. It was strange to see him on the stage, but I had to admit he was good.

Dennis joined the army during the Vietnam War and was stationed as an MP (military police) in Germany. He was assigned to the US federal prison in Frankfurt and has a number of stories about how vicious the inmates of that prison were. These prisoners were hardened and mean and were not to be trusted. He and his fellow MPs knew how to deal with them, and they had to take action many times.

When he was discharged, he went to work in our Uncle Jack's family shoe store in Sayville and eventually bought it. It was a store that specialized in children's shoes but also had men's and ladies' shoes.

Dennis by then was married to Linda, and they had two children, Deirdre and Evan. I will tell you more about that family in a little bit, but again, I don't want to get ahead of myself. Dennis and I were and still are very close, seeing each other quite often.

Seventh Son

Donald "Deefer" Mahoney, born the seventh son—I was the baby boy, and to be honest, I was probably a little spoiled until my sister came along. My nickname was the result of my uncles calling their brother Donald (my namesake), D for Donald, shortening that to Deefer. My nickname was typically used by the immediate family only until I got into high school. As I said, Dennis and I were close, and he was just ahead of me in St. Patrick's and also Bay Shore High School. We were both friends with Ned, and he heard one of my uncles call me Deefer when he was visiting our home one day. He questioned them, and it was from then on I was known to everyone as Deefer. Whenever he would see me in the hall at school, he would holler at the top of his lungs, "DEEFER!" Everybody called me Deefer from then on.

I played sports in school, including wrestling and football. I wasn't a great wrestler, but I could play football. We had a great football team, and when I say *team*, I mean every player was good. We were well coached in the junior varsity program by Coaches Allen and Jones, and by the time we were all on varsity, we really didn't need a coach.

Coach Dave was also a wrestling coach and was very funny. One of the wrestlers on our team was Richey Debois, a good wrestler. Coach Dave called him Da boys, not being able to pronounce the French version. We were getting on a bus to go to a meet, and he asked, "Where's Da boys?"

Billy, another wisecrack friend, said, "The boys are on the bus!"

He would train us really hard and was one of the reasons we were so good. Practices were sometimes held on the baseball field, and he would joke after making us run wind sprints that if we had to puke, the baseball coach didn't want us puking on second base and to run out to the outfield fence if we were going to hurl.

Our team just clicked, and for three out of four years I played, our team was undefeated, and in our senior year, we won what was called The Rutgers Cup that was known as the Long Island Champion. I started on every defense team as a middle linebacker with a good friend of mine, Bobby Cox, whose father was a high school football coach in another town close to Bay Shore. Other teams rarely scored on us, and our offense could and did run the score up so quick, the second offensive team would come into play almost every game. I was a backup running back, but our running backs were so much faster. Our starting running back was Googoo Powell. He was small but quick and strong and could change direction and cut on a dime. It was rare for me to be put in as a running back, but I was on every other team, kickoff team, kickoff return team, punting team, punt return team, defense, so I was on the field a lot. I loved playing football and wore the same jersey number in honor of my brother Terry, hoping I could be as good a player as he was. When my brother Mooncat was on leave from the Marine Corps, he got a chance to see me play one of my last games before he went to war.

Playing sports did take its toll on my body, and I am paying for it as I age. I injured my knee while playing touch football at Windsor Field one day and continue to have problems with it to this day. I didn't tell the coach how I got injured because he would have benched me. The doctor wanted to operate on it, but in those days, it was extreme, not the arthroscopic, easier procedures done nowadays. I refused and was back playing two weeks later after my own rehab. I just loved playing football. After high school, I was asked to play semipro for a team that had started on Long Island, but I was afraid I would get injured, and they didn't provide insurance, and I had to go to work. They only paid a couple hundred dollars a game anyway. That team disbanded after a couple of seasons.

During my youth, I was always on the beach, whether it was Benji's beach or the beach on the town of Islip on Fire Island called Atlantique Beach, with the bay on one side and a walk to the Atlantic Ocean on the other side. To get there, you had to take a slow big old ferry across the bay called the *Fire Island Queen* that took in what it seemed like forever to get there. Many people think that Fire Island was only for gay people, but there were many family communities on the island and only two communities that attracted the gay community, Cherry Grove and the Fire Island Pines. We called the *Queen* the slow boat to China, but it took us to a family beach run by the Town of Islip.

Growing Up

Dennis and I had sibling rivalry when we were young and would have fistfight all the time. I would tell people I learned how to fight before I could walk. With six older brothers, it was necessary. If you didn't know how to fight, your food would be gone before you had a chance.

We got into a battle in the narrow kitchen one day when we were teenagers, and Jackson PDQ came in and grabbed us each and held one of us on one wall, the other on the opposite, with our feet not even touching the floor until we cooled down. He was strong as hell.

It was on the beach when I was still attending St. Pat's that I met a girl who I didn't know would change my life.

Her name was Donna. When I finally ended up going to high school, Donna was there. We kind of avoided each other at first, but she was a cheerleader, so we saw each other often at sporting events at school. It turned out she was Linda's sister. Linda ended up dating and married to my brother Dennis.

I tried to pretend I didn't like her by teasing her, and because she was this beautiful redhead, I would call her Red Beast to piss her off. Before you get angry at me, it was because I was trying to hide the fact that I loved her. Eventually, I married her. It was a stupid adolescent reaction to someone you really liked, like stupid adolescent boys would do.

We didn't date until she went off to college, but she told me later in our relationship that she fell in love with me the first time we met—a sweet love story that makes me gag. Anyway, the funny part of that story is my brother dated Linda all through high school and went off into the army. When he got back and Donna and I got married, their father finally went to Dennis after he was dating Linda for so long and asked him, "When are you going to marry my daughter?" They did marry, but it was after I married Donna. Before you think it's weird that brothers married sisters, it wasn't like the mountains in West Virginia where sisters marry brothers! That's just wrong on every level.

We got along together so good that after we were married and started careers, we ended up purchasing an old Victorian-style home together in Sayville, Long Island. More to come on that.

I attended Saint Patrick parochial school from kindergarten to eighth grade. My brothers preceded me and my sister after me.

Saint Pat's, as we called it, was run by Saint Patrick's Church, a beautiful building across the street from St. Pat's campus. The teachers were nuns and wore the full garb covering everything except their face. It was strict in terms of behavior and was probably responsible for how disciplined I became later in life, but I struggled to behave the way they wanted me to. I remember my first experience was meeting the Mother Superior (that's what they called the mother superior, head nun, or principal), and she said, "Oh, you're a Mahoney? We've been waiting for you!"—ominous threat. I didn't disappoint. I found it to be as if I was in a prisoner of war camp.

We walked to school most days; bad weather, including rain, snow, and wind, didn't matter. We had to make it a mile and a half to two miles or so before the bell rang. If you got there early enough, you could play a few minutes before the first bell rang, which signaled to get in line for whatever grade you were in. When the second bell rang, it meant you had to be totally quiet, no talking at all. Third bell, you follow in line, marching to your classroom. I never got along with any of my nun teachers, except one, for the nine years I attended, Sister Mary Adelaid, who later on became a principal of a school further east on Long Island.

If you didn't follow the rules, it was capital punishment. I was punished quite often. When you filed into the classroom, you had to enter the cloak room through a closet door, hang up you coat and book bag, and proceed through the door into the classroom to your desk. I had a nun one time when I misbehaved bring me into the cloak room, shut the door, turn off the light, and start swinging, beating the crap out of me! Sister Antonio—she was built like a man and even had a mustache. Nuns would use weapons too like the pointer made of hickory used to smack your knuckles if your spelling or handwriting wasn't up to standard or get whacked with one of the large erasers that were normally used for cleaning the chalk off the chalkboard. It had a wooden back on it to grip and was used if you talked when you weren't supposed to. Look, I'm not saying sometimes I didn't deserve being punished, but sometimes, it was taken too far.

I remember once in line during a fire drill, lining up to march out of the building, someone was talking. Antonio swung around and beat the crap out of Mary, knocking her to the ground. One of the other girls confessed, "Sister, it wasn't Mary. It was me talking." Mary took the beating in stride.

I begged my mother on my knees, "Mom, please take me out of this school."

Her response was, "All your brothers went to that school, and you are going to finish too."

The nuns were big on humility, and I remember having to walk to school one morning in a snowstorm. Because I didn't wear snow boots on the way, my shoes and the bottoms of my pants got soaked. To teach me a lesson, she made me stand at the head of the class to humiliate me. It didn't, just taught me anger instead.

I did make it through and finally made to Bay Shore High School. Everybody knew you came from St. Pat's because if you raised your hand to answer a question and a teacher called on you and you stood up to answer, the rest of the class would start laughing. You could answer without standing up? That took me a bit to get used to. I hadn't experienced that kind of freedom in school, but I started to take advantage of that freedom. More troublemaking to follow. If you played sports at Bay Shore, you were sort of allowed to get away with breaking some rules. I played football with a fellow named Richey. His mother was the front desk supervisor. Because you were on the team with her son, if you wanted a pass, she would sign it and give it to you, and we would sneak off campus. (Everyone kept that secret, and it wasn't all the players, just the ones who were close to her son.)

    We would usually go to a little strip mall with a candy, soda shop, a pizza place, and a few other stores. The name of the store area was Crossroads because it intersected with two roads. We would go to Crossroads and play the pinball machine till it was time for a class that if the teacher didn't see you, alarms would go off. We had a vice principal, Mr. Thieben (pronounced T-Ben). He was the school disciplinarian. When we would be at Crossroads, we always had a lookout, and one day, the lookout hollered, "T-Ben, T-Ben!" We all looked for a place to hide. We were busted! He punished but was always fair, especially if you played sports because at one time, he had a brief career in the NBA. He was probably six feet six with a shaved bald head, looking very intimidating, but almost everyone liked him. He had these long fingers that were like steel rods, and he would poke you in the chest with his forefinger. "Mr. Mahoney, I'm very unhappy with your behavior!" He fit the punishment to the crime. He knew all the Mahoneys.

Eighth Sibling

Regina (Gina-Beena) was the eighth child born. Everyone said my mother kept trying until she had a daughter. Gina was as tough as any of her brothers, but she was beautiful. When I think of Gina, I know it was tough on her having so many older brothers, especially when she graduated from St. Patrick's and went to high school. She also had to wear a uniform at St. Pat's. When she got to high school, none of the boys wanted to date her or take her out. They were too afraid of her older brothers, including me! I was fine with that, but she finally started to date when they saw how she stood up to us. The one guy who wasn't afraid of us was another neighbor, Doug Brewster. His family owned the second largest boatyard on the south shore of Long Island named Brewster's Shipyard. Doug was all right with all of us. Gina had the Mahoney sense of humor and would repeat a story to people when I was with her.

Apparently, when she was born, I got very jealous of the attention she was getting. I was after all, until she showed up, the baby boy receiving all the attention. She couldn't even talk yet but claims she remembers it vividly when she was placed in her playpen so Mom could do some chores. I would sneak over and pinch her to make her cry. Mom would come into the room and say, "What's wrong, honey?" When she calmed down and Mom got distracted again, I would sneak right back and pinch her again! Mom would rush back in and say again, "What's wrong, baby?" She remembered I did that to her for her entire life and had a great sense of humor about it and swore she would someday get even with me for that. We grew up together and had some of the same friends our whole life.

Gina married Doug and had a son, Doug Junior. I am his godfather. Doug and Gina lived at Fire Island on the bay side in the

Brewster family compound called The Eel Farm. After years of raising their son, things eventually didn't work out, and they eventually separated and divorced. I am sure it was tough for all of them, but they stayed friendly.

Gina eventually remarried another good guy named Phil Porter, and they had a daughter, Shannon.

I was close to Doug but also to Phil. Great times with both. Doug and Phil would even play golf together occasionally.

Life, Family, Friends, and Adventures

Being friends with Jerry since grammar school, we visit him and his wife, Lori, as often as we can. They live in Montauk. I have had a wonderful and fulfilling life with great family and friends. I had multiple work experiences that gave me my life education. When I was a kid, I started to make some change pulling weeds from neighbor's gardens. That didn't last very long; it was too boring. For a short time, I delivered newspapers. Kids back then would have these huge baskets over the front wheel in front of handlebars filled with newspapers for delivering to homes that had a subscription to that paper. I did that for a summer until a mishap. Normally, you would just toss the paper up onto the homes' steps or porch every day. Once a week, you would need to collect from the homeowners what they owed for delivery. An older woman was in her home, and when I knocked, a big German shepherd came to the door. When she opened the door, she couldn't hold the dog, and he bolted out the door slamming into my chest and knocking me right over the porch rails into the bushes. He just kept on running like it was a jail break. I don't remember if I collected or not, but I was done delivering newspapers.

Most of our spare time was spent at Benji's beach swimming and diving in the bay as it was a short walk to the beach and the dock on the bay. If we weren't swimming, we were fishing right off the dock with cane poles using shiners as bait to catch all species of fish, snapper bluefish, flounder, weakfish, blowfish, etc. We would go fishing a lot at daybreak, and if we caught blowfish (some people called them puffers because their defense was gasping air and expanding their bellies to avoid being swallowed), we would bring our catch back to the house and cut the backs out and grill them on our outdoor grill. These fish were delicious, and you could hold them in your hand and eat the meat off, just like eating a chicken leg. Great childhood memories!

We would have the first outdoor summer barbeque on my birthday, May 9, because the weather was usually warming up enough to cook and eat out in the backyard. The neighborhood kids would come after we caught fish and grilled them and corn on the cob right on the coals.

Eventually, they built the Bay Shore Marina and eliminated the dock we fished at, and that kind of ruined fishing in that area of the bay forever. There was some bad things about building the marina: it increased not only the fishing but also traffic past our home, with all the floating docks and boat ramps they installed for the multiple boats and boat owners.

There was some good things about the marina. At the end of the marina, they built a fuel dock, fishing gear and bait store, and a food counter. When I was in high school, I got a job at the marina, fueling boats and loading ice, beer, drinks, bait, etc. on all types of boats including big sport fishing vessels. The tips were great for a kid. I made a lot of cash that I just pissed away mostly on beer for me and my friends! Yes, I started drinking beer at an early age; everyone in my group of friends did (naughty)!

I witnessed some strange happenings at the marina. One day, a man pulled up in a brand new Cadillac convertible and jumped out the door to run inside and buy something, and before he went in, he realized the car was still running. When he reached back in to shut it off and grab the keys, he accidentally hit the car in gear, and it took off the end of the dock right into the middle of the channel and watched it sink. They had to get a crane to pull it from the middle of the channel. Another time a woman with a handicap hit the gas instead of the break by mistake, and her car shot over right onto an outboard boat at one of the floating docks and sank it, and her car began to sink. Lucky for her, a group of lifeguards from Benji's beach were having lunch at the counter, and they jumped in and pulled her out of the sinking car.

They held The Bay Shore Mako Shark Fishing Tournament every year at the Marina. It was sponsored by the Bay Shore Yacht Club. When at its peak, hundreds of entries would pull in for a long weekend for the weighing in. There would be days when we would weigh thousands of huge sharks, sometimes weighing over a thousand pounds. I remember one weekend with 1,500 fish being weighed. Some of the big fish would have to be lifted with a crane to weigh them.

The process was each boat was issued a number that they had to post on side of the boat and would radio us as they would be getting close to dock. We kept pretty good track of them because of limiting docking space to make sure everyone was checked before time limits expired. The first thing we would do is ask the captain if the fish was dead to make sure for safe handling when pulling them onto the dock to weigh them. I would ask one captain if his fish was dead, and he would say yes. I would proceed to grab the fish by the nose and dorsal fin to slide the fish off the boat. One time, a fish wasn't dead and proceeded to snap at me! So we put a 1x1 stick in its mouth, and it snapped as if it was a twig. Needless to say, I made that captain wait until every other boat and fish was checked in before we weighed it.

They always had a handful of marine biologists on the dock to take data and samples. One day, a blue shark had babies on the dock. We had floating bait pens that were filled with live killies (bait fish) to sell to local fishermen. The marine biologist asked us to put the shark's babies in the pens to keep them alive, telling us they wouldn't eat them because they were too young. That was a lie, but just being kids, we believed them. When the owner of the marina showed up, he almost had a heart attack. I haven't listened to anything since then without being skeptical. Thousands of dollars of bait could have been eaten.

I learned a lot about fishing from those days. My Dad fished a lot and would take us with him from time to time. He had a close friend, Bill Entenmann from Entenmann's bakery. The Entenmanns had a local bakery that the brothers took over when they were old enough and grew it into a national bakery outfit that you can see in supermarkets to this day. They were just normal hardworking people who knew how to market, good family and really nice people. If you had met them, you would never know how wealthy they had become. Bill had bought a sport fishing boat and would invite my father all the time to go fishing with him. They took me all the time. For some reason, I think they thought I was a lucky charm because they always caught fish when I was on board. They had a great captain. Years later, they changed their interest into horses and had a farm where they raised thoroughbreds. They didn't abandon boats altogether and had a custom sailboat being built in South Florida. It was massive, and they had planned to launch it and wanted Jackson to come down for the maiden voyage. We were concerned because Jackson had gotten pretty ill by then, but Bill insisted and said if he has a problem or a turn, he would have a helicopter pick him up to take him to the hospital. He wanted Jack there.

I have been around boats and fishing my whole life. The best fisherman I knew in those days was Doug Brewster. I fished with Doug all the time also. We fished the Mako tournament more than a few times and always did pretty good. One time we were fishing, and I was on one side of the boat, and Doug was on the bow of the boat. We had sharks swimming all around the boat. Doug started to move from the bow past the cabin to get to the rear when I heard a splash. I turned around, and Doug was standing on deck soaking wet. It turned out, he lost his footing, and in the time it took me to turn around, he had gotten out of the water and was standing on the deck. All sharks do is swim, eat, and make baby sharks, and he didn't want to be a meal!

Eventually, they stopped the tournament to let the local shark population recover. I have definite feelings about fish populations that in my opinion and years of experience, the populations are cyclical, just like climate, etc. I see fish populations decrease and increase at an approximate ten-year cycle. Doug and I for a short time did some gill fishing for weakfish in the bay and sold them to local restaurants, primarily on Fire Island. The government overreach eventually outlawed gill fishing. Before they ended gill fishing, we would box up our catch and run them to the different restaurants on Fire Island. One day, the weather was way too rough to run across the bay fast enough to get to the restaurants, so we borrowed one of the boats we had access to at the yard. It was one of the fastest cigarette-style boats that could normally get across the bay in fifteen minutes. We loaded the boxes of fish into the cabin and took off. We made it across the bay in time, but it was so rough, and the boat bounced so much, the tops of the boxes came loose and the fish poured out into the white leather-covered seats before we realized it was happening. It took us days to clean that boat, and the smell never really went away. The owner never noticed it.

What I experienced as the biggest threat to fishing was pollution caused by sewage leaks and also some of the large corporate Chinese and Japanese trawler companies who for years were fishing in our waters. Also, I saw the building of the Bay Shore Marina destroy habitats for not only fish but also the clam industry, which was a huge industry in the Great South Bay. Combine that with clam dredge companies putting the local bay men basically out of business. I knew many of these clam diggers; as a matter of fact, my sister Gina's husband, Phil, was one for a while. The little man has no chance against the government regulators and conglomerates that lobby for their special interest. Crooks!

Some of the local one-man clammers resorted to breaking the law to make a living by getting high-speed boats and clamming in illegal waters. They would make sure their boats were black or dark colored and could outrun the law when they did try to catch them. The law responded by getting faster boats, but that didn't work too well because these men knew the bay better than anyone, and they would just make sure they were chased where they could run aground whoever was chasing them. That didn't last long as the law eventually took to helicopters to catch them. That pretty much put them out of business. It was a dangerous process with these pirate clammers digging at night in polluted areas where the clams were plentiful, putting the public in danger of receiving bad shellfish.

The biggest damage in my view to that industry is the leasing program to these big corporations using large dredging vessels to dredge up all the clams that would have been the areas where the single honest clam diggers could have harvested those clams without destroying the environment that the dredges do destroy! The silt from these dredges just coat the bottom killing off growth of other organisms that feed smaller life forms and preventing more species from populating. Common sense, but government doesn't have any. Overregulating by these government agencies needs some overhauling, and someone needs to put a stop to the runaway control these agencies have.

Neighborhood, Neighbors, and Friends

The neighborhood we grew up in was full of families, so we had lots of friends we would hang with, play with, and get in trouble with. When we weren't at school, we were constantly at the beach or playing football or baseball, always outdoors by choice or force by our parents. I can't tell you how many times our parents would tell us to go out and play: "Come home for lunch, and make sure you're back in the house when the streetlights come on." In the winter, when it was freezing out, we would walk to the lakes to go skating. The neighborhood had small- to medium-sized homes for the most part but had many old estate homes that were used prior to the war for the owners that would come out from the city to spend time in the country, but after the war, most of them were abandoned. We played ball in the huge yards that these abandoned estates were on. One was named Shanley's, and we played both football and baseball on that field. When we played baseball, the field was long, and then there was a wooded area that was considered a homerun if you hit the ball into the woods on the fly. The estate home was to the right of where we set up home plate but was not regulation distance from where we would put first base. We had a ground rule that if you hit the ball up on one of the four-story porches, it would be considered a ground rule double. The team that was fielding when that happened would have to climb to retrieve the ball. Baseballs were considered pretty inexpensive in those days, but not for kids. We would pool our change just to buy one, so we had to make sure we retrieved them from the woods or one of the porches. Sometimes the woods won. We all would wear baseball caps and have gloves that were either birthday or Christmas gifts, but other equipment wasn't used, like catcher masks or chest protectors. We had to make another rule because one time, when I was playing catcher and the batter hit the ball, he tossed the bat back and hit me square in the forehead, creating a massive lump and near-knocking me out. A new rule was adopted for if you hit the ball and did not just drop the bat you were out. Man, those days were fun!

We played in these abandoned estate properties all the time. Another estate was the Rockenbell's estate. The house was this huge Gothic-style home with turret-style towers and huge rooms. No one ever discouraged us from playing on those properties, but I know our parents didn't want us in the buildings, but that always didn't stop us. We would sneak in and go up to the top floor, and it had a laundry chute that would end up in the bottom floor. I can't remember who attempted it first; it was probably Murphy, but it was a fun ride down the chute! You couldn't be a fat kid and do it.

There were also some big hills of dirt from clearing scattered around the property that we would slide down or if it had snowed would sled down. One Christmas, I got a Rifleman rifle from Santa. *The Rifleman* was an old Western television show starring Chuck Conners, and he had a special rifle with a hoop around the trigger that you could swing about before pulling the trigger. Old repeats of that show are still aired on some of the nostalgic channels even today. My brother Mike asked me to try it when we were playing at Rockenbell's, but when he jumped off one of the hills with it, he snapped it in half. I cried like a little baby.

One night, we heard fire engine sirens and went outside to see the building in flames. I am pretty sure it was arson but nobody we knew. We wouldn't destroy one of our favorite places. There were some bad boys from blocks away, and we all kind of thought we knew who it could have been. That fire burned for two days—sad day.

Brightwaters was part of Bay Shore that had a collection of shallow lakes that would freeze in winter months. It was pretty close to where we lived especially if you cut through some property known as Okatee. We ice-skated and played ice hockey, and it gave us another thing to look forward to do when not playing ball. One of the lakes had a small waterfall called cascades at the edge of the lake, where it would rarely freeze near it. We were playing hockey, and the puck went over close to the cascade, and when I skated over to retrieve it, I lost my edge and fell. The ice was thin, and I crashed through it. It wasn't deep, but the only part of my body that didn't get wet was my right arm. I had to walk back to the house in the freezing cold weather. I had a hell of a time trying to climb over the fence of the shortcut. When I finally made it home, no one was there. I went into the back door and struggled to get my jeans off, which were frozen solid. When I slid them off, they slid across the kitchen floor. I stood in front of our gas heater for more than half an hour.

We spent many days skating at the lakes. I would meet Donna there most times, and she told me that once when her mother came to pick her up, she asked, "Who was that nice Italian boy you were talking to?" I always was very tan from spending so much time outside, so she assumed I was Italian from my dark olive skin color.

One of our friends and neighbors was a boy named Anthony Falbo. Anthony was a big strong fellow. I was amazed at how he could drink a bottle quart of milk at once when he was thirsty from playing outside. His mom spoke little English, but man, was she a great cook! When we were outside playing around suppertime, we would hear her holler out the front door, "Anthony, manja!" and he would go running at full speed—good friend and family.

Bay Shore was a great place to grow up. We could walk to downtown from our house. At the corner of main street and Clinton Avenue was a candy and soda shop named Oscar's. If we had a little extra change, we would tell Mom, "We're going to Oscar's!"

Oscar would follow you around the store to make sure no one was stealing comic books, candy, or baseball cards. It was right across from Saint Patrick's church and school. On the other corner to the west was the Bay Shore movie theater. This theater was a beautiful Gothic-style building with plush seating and crystal chandelier lights hanging from the ceiling. It was impressive just to look around at the architecture.

To be honest, we would pool our money to get one of us into a movie, and they would wait until the ushers weren't paying attention and sneak us into a back door. This had to happen quick so as not to get caught. I think sometimes, the ushers knew but let it slide because we were all fairly poor. We saw all the best movies ever in that theater. There was a second theater down the east end of the main street called The Regent. It was a dinghy, dirty place, and we rarely attended shows there. Eventually, it turned into an X-rated theater at the beginning of the deterioration of downtown businesses. Downtown Bay Shore had thriving businesses up and down the main street and even the side streets, but then they built the South Shore Mall, and the people who used to shop downtown would go to the mall for cheaper prices, and that was what started to put the small-shop owners out of business.

Another thing that hurt was when they started to house many of the war veterans into the area. It was easy for the government to release them into the population and house them in some of the old, abandoned buildings that were around the neighborhood. These guys were pretty much harmless, but some people were afraid of them. Most of them were suffering from PTSD; everyone back then called it shell shock. They really didn't bother us as kids, but we were kind of mean, giving them nicknames. I remember one: his name was Herman, and he would stand on the corner, clicking his heels together and rocking back and forth and saying out loud, "Kafadeeda, kafadeeda." We never figured out what that meant. If you walked past him, he would try and grub cigarettes. "Got a cigarette?" he would say to anyone who walked past him. Most of these guys were harmless, just suffering from the effects of war.

While in high school, when off from school, we would all meet in Brightwaters at a big field called Windsor Field and play touch football. One day, my brother Mike drove up and said to me, "Get in." I did. He was pissed about something, and when I asked him what I did, he didn't respond. I was trying to think what I did that would get me in trouble he would know about, but nothing came to mind. We drove downtown to a department store named Grants, and he took me straight up to the manager's office. Some kid I went to grammar school with got caught shoplifting and told them, knowing my brothers were cops, he was Donald Mahoney, thinking he would get away with it. Mike wasn't pissed at me. He was pissed at that kid for using my name. I told him who the kid was. That kid was shaking and crying, fearing more for what I might do to him than the store.

Ocean, swimming, water skiing, fishing, and clamming were regular activities for us all. I learned how to swim in summer at an early age from my brothers. It was a must to learn because of all the water around us all the time just to be able to stay safe. My brothers Pat, Mike, Terry, and Brian took us down to the canal next to our grandmother's house and threw me and Dennis in and yelled at us to kick our legs and flap our arms to get to the side and climb up. Once you got up, they threw you in again and again. They all could swim, and Patrick and Terry were lifeguards, so we weren't too afraid or really in danger after the first time. They kept it up for days until we improved enough so that they didn't have to worry about us. That sort of thing made our generation tough.

Jackson PDQ would sit watching ball games in his easy chair by the front door when he was home. He made it clear for us to use the back door to come in and out of the house so as not disturb whatever game he was watching. Terry and Patrick would spend the summers diving off the high boards and platforms. Terry was the athletic diver, and Patrick was more graceful. Terry could do a dive they called a half gainer, and he did one off the high board, but some friend missed him doing it and asked him to do it again. On Terry's second attempt, he came too close to the board and hit his chin, knocking his front teeth out. Ouch! We called him Toophy until he got false teeth to replace them. He would laugh his evil laugh.

Patrick was on the high platform another time, goofing around with his buddies and fell off onto the dock below and broke both his arms. He walked home to the house, and because his arms were broken, he kicked on the front door to get PDQ to open the door. Jackson yelled out, "Go around the back." They set his broken arms, and it wasn't too long after that both he and Terry were back diving. I think too many accidents were starting to happen, so they eventually dismantled the high dives and platforms.

I was a tough kid growing up, having learned how to fight at an early age from my brothers. I had a mean streak too, not backing down from bullies. Because of my tough upbringing and attitude, I was constantly being challenged by someone who thought they could beat me. I rarely lost a fight even to somebody bigger because I was more of a street fighter. As a kid, a tenant who lived behind my grandmother taught me how to box, and toward the end of high school, I would spar with my friend Billy, who planned to join the marines and box on the marine boxing team. I remember Billy was training and asked me to spar with him, but it was right after I was in a car accident and broke my jaw and shattered my cheekbone. We had been driving at night near the high school, and it just started raining. We were in a Chevy Corvair. They were cars that had a trunk in the front and an engine in the rear that made them dangerous. A couple of "hoods" were walking in the middle of the street wearing all black, and the driver didn't see them until the last second, swerved, lost control, and hit a tree. I was in the death seat and hit the dash and broke my jaw in three places and shattered my cheekbone. We had just picked up a case of beer, and all the bottles broke, and beer was all over the back. The four of us tried to throw the remains out before the police came and caught the underage drinkers. That didn't work. I recovered and have a funny story about my hospital stay I will tell later.

To get back to sparring with Billy, he assured me he wouldn't hit me in the face, so I agreed. While sparring, I saw an opening and popped him in the nose. Something snapped in him, and he wailed on my body not once hitting me in the face. Billy did end up boxing for the marines. What I learned in street fighting to win was, if you know this bully is going to hit you, hit him hard in the nose first! Billy played football with me, and he was the most disciplined man I knew. He would also wrestle and during wrestling season would lose a bunch of weight to be able to wrestle at a lower-weight class and gain the weight back the following football season.

When I was recovering in the hospital with my broken jaw, I had just gotten a shot for pain when I heard a knock on the window. My room was on the third or fourth floor, but I looked over and saw a guy I played football with, Butter Butticovoli, standing on the fire escape. He lived right behind the hospital and had climbed up the fire escape with a six pack of beer to visit me! I said, "Butter, I am on medication. I can't drink," but he said the beer is for him and sat and drank it—crazy guy, good football player.

Sometimes, I would walk home from football practice. Our home was probably five miles or so from the high school, and I would walk past the local bar and hangout that all my brothers would go to called The Mystic Inn. This place was owned by the Di Natali's. Doo-Doo was the brother that ran it. He had brothers that had other bars in Bay Shore. When I would walk by, Doo-Doo would say to me, "Mahoney, don't even think about coming in here. I know when your birthday is." Legal drinking age was eighteen back then. It did become our regular hangout when I turned eighteen. That's not to say we didn't go to other bars in other towns when underage, actually the first time when I was sixteen.

The Mystic was a bucket of blood with fights just about every night. I had an issue one night with some guy thinking I had an interest in him that kept asking me if he could buy me a drink. Draw your own conclusions. I said no, but this guy kept it up, and after about the third time brushing up against me, I blasted him and kicked his ass. I beat his ass pretty bad, and he left bleeding with a swollen face. A few days later, I was walking past the local pool room. You could find some unsavory people hanging out there, but I knew most of them. One guy I knew from school told me the guy I beat up was an actor that had an older brother that was connected. Yes, connected, and he was asking around about me. This guy told me I should hide out for a couple of weeks, so I did. Nothing ever happened from it.

One night, we were all there celebrating when Mooncat had returned from Viet Nam. My friend Gerry was there with his brother, Danny, who was friends with my brother Mooncat and had been wounded in combat and had lost his sight. All of a sudden, the doors busted open, both the front and back door, stopping anyone from escaping, and in rushed a motorcycle gang called The Pagans. This gang was more brutal than The Hells Angels, and they would travel around Long Island, picking what they thought was the toughest bar in different towns. Big mistake! The fight erupted with fists flying, bottles and cue sticks breaking over people's heads, and bodies being thrown about. Danny backed up against a wall and just started swinging his cane. I remember his cane just swishing though the air. We beat the crap out of them and a lot of us, and they ended up at the local hospital. They never came back. That was my first run-in with the Pagans. They picked the wrong town and the wrong time. Dennis and I would go to the Mystic a lot because our friend Ned tended bar there. It was always entertaining when Ned was working, sometimes three or four deep at the bar. Ned would get a break in the middle of his shift, and the three of us would sneak around the corner to a lesbian bar called Pat and Scotty's. They loved Ned, and they treated us like friends, and we laughed the whole time we were there. Those were fun times.

There was a second time we ran into the Pagans. Doug had a house down South Florida at Singer Island, and we all went on vacation, and Doug and I entered a shark fishing contest out of West Palm Beach along with a friend of his, Ben. At the time, Doug owned a sixteen-foot open-skiff wooden hulled outboard manufactured by Eltro. One morning, before we got out of bed, we heard a blood-curdling scream from Gina. She had gone into the garage to throw trash away, and an animal hissed loudly at her, scaring the shit out of her with her scream scaring the hell out of the rest of us. Doug grabbed his shotgun and took the can and tossed it onto the beach. Nothing. He kicked the can and outran a possum hissing with his teeth bared running right at Doug. *Kaboom!* No more possum.

We left to go shark fishing. To get to deep-enough water out of West Palm inlet only took about fifteen minutes. We fished all morning catching sailfish, wahoo, and barracuda. Doug's friend was holding the wahoo up for a photo when the fish's head snapped back and took a chunk out of his belly. He was wearing a white bathing suit, and the blood just gushed all down it. Then that afternoon, we caught three hammerhead sharks—one bigger than the other. The one I hooked into weighed out to 589 pounds and was twelve feet long. The boat was only sixteen feet, and we had to lash the fish to the side and just crawl back to the dock. We had to tow the fish back in time for weigh in, and it took us five hours to make it back to the dock just in time to make the deadline. The looks we got from fisherman who thought they had won was priceless. *Look at these Yankees cruising in and winning our tournament at the last minute.* The grand prize was a Yamaha 250 CC dirt bike, and I had it shipped back to New York.

That set up the future meeting with the Pagans. We would get a group of guys with dirt bikes and haul them to the east end at Montauk, where there was a huge open field you could pull into that had trails going five miles in either direction. We were in the field preparing to ride the trails when we heard a loud rumbling noise approaching the field, and in came approximately forty Pagans with their bitches on the back. One fat big biker with ink up and down his body said about my brand new dirt bike, "Nice scooter! You mind if I ride it?"

Using my best judgment, I said, "Sure." I hadn't even ridden it yet. His big ass got on the bike and revved it up, and the torque on the bike grabbed and took off, sliding his fat ass bouncing on the ground and the rear wheel just hopping down the trail until it crashed.

He said, "Oh, sorry, man."

The bike wasn't destroyed, and I rode it that whole summer until I broke a spark plug off on a stump in the middle of the woods that took me all day to get back to a road to go home. Donna didn't know I was out riding, and she asked me to sell it, and I did. I would have eventually got killed or killed myself on it anyway because I was reckless.

When we were younger, we would swim in the bay, and occasionally, our folks would drive us to Jones's beach or Robert Moses to the ocean. Jones's beach had a huge Olympic-size pool with platform diving and high boards back then, and I started to jump off the platforms and diving boards but didn't learn how to dive yet. We would just watch Pat and Terry and some of the other men who were also good at diving. We were all water rats, in the ocean or the bay all the time. I learned how to water ski when I was young. When we got older, Doug Brewster and some of our friends built a ski jump at the eel farm in front of his mother and father's house. They had a T-dock sticking out in the bay with deck chairs so the adults could sit on chairs and watch boaters go by and have cocktail hour.

We built the ski jump from marine plywood and fiberglassed it. When we glassed it was the process of pouring resin over the fiber with a number of coats. It wasn't finished with what is called gel coat to make the surface completely smooth like the finish on a surfboard or a fiberglass boat.

We started to get really good at jumping to the point we started to get cocky with trick jumping like twisting in the air when you went off the end of the jump. One of our friends, Glen, was a daredevil, so he wanted to jump on one ski called a slalom ski. That wasn't something no one in those days had attempted but nowadays is a normal thing in competitive water skiing. The problem with Glen attempting this trick was this slalom ski had a skeg on it like surfboards have for making it easier to cut back and forth. When he hit the jump, the skeg made him fall on his side, and he didn't let go of the tow rope and got pulled across the unfinished jump, peeling the skin off from his arm down his side and legs. Saltwater made it more painful. Glen didn't give up and did it eventually. He was a trendsetter. It started to get too easy for all of us to jump the ski jump the way it was set up, so Doug decided we should raise it up to make longer higher jumps. We just put one more cinder block under the jump. Guess who volunteered to try it first. Me! When the towboat swung around towing me toward the jump, all the old folks were sitting on the deck watching us. I saw the jump as I approached, and raising it made it look like a wall. When I hit it, I shot straight up in the air and hollered out loud, "Oh shit!" I hit the water on my back, and when I did, the skis closed on my neck like a pair of scissors bruising both sides of my neck. We lowered it back after that. I was lucky it didn't decapitate me.

Jobs, Marriages, and Residences

I did get a job driving a taxi in the summer months from the train station to the ferry terminal for a short time, running back and forth to the station with a bunch of city idiots going to Fire Island and made good money for a young kid. The one thing the owner of the taxi company required was you had to pick up a night shift one time a week. I had a couple of problems doing that. The cars were not like city cabs with barricades between the driver and the passengers. One night, I was dispatched to pick up a fare in what was a questionable neighborhood on a dead-end street. I was a little bit fooled because when I pulled up to the address, this guy came out of the screened-in porch of the house. I learned later the house was empty. He jumped in the back seat and slid right behind me. I automatically had a bad feeling, and so I purposely turned around to look backward and back down the street instead of turning the car around. I knew something was wrong, and I wanted to make sure I got a good look at this guy. He was a thin black guy with protruding buck teeth that was easy to identify. When I got back to the end of the street and started to drive forward, he pulled out the gun and stuck it to the back of my head and told me to stop the car and get out. I did, and his two accomplices ran up and pushed me onto the hood and demanded my cash. I forked it over, and as I pulled the cash out, my ID, license, etc. fell out on the ground, and they didn't see it. They told me to run down the street, and I did. I knew they weren't going to shoot me. I ran a few houses away and knocked on a door and explained to the homeowner what had happened, and they called the police for me. That really didn't scare me because I figured they weren't going to shoot me in the middle of a neighborhood, but the next time did scare me.

I picked a fare up at a local bar, and I got that bad feeling again expecting something to happen. It's funny how that sixth sense does work. This guy slid in behind me again and reached over the seat to grab me. He had a knife in his hand, and when he reached, I grabbed both his wrists, felt the knife, and took it out of his hand. I really felt as if he was going to stick me, but my adrenaline wouldn't let him, and I turned around to stick it in him! He slid back and jumped out. I jumped out to catch him but, in my haste, had left the car in gear, and it started to take off. I hesitated a second, and he got away. I jumped in the car and stopped it. That was the end of taxi driving for me.

My brothers put together a plan to catch the three guys with the gun by putting undercover cops as drivers with a cop hiding in the back seat. I can't tell you exactly how they caught them, but they did. They brought me in to view a lineup, and I picked the guy out right away. It turned out one of his partners was someone I went to in high school with. They all went away for a long time. I never caught the guy with the knife.

Donna and I got married when I was twenty-one, and Dennis and Linda got married not to long after. Donna found an apartment for me and her near the house I was raised in. I was by this time working at the shipyard with Doug. I loved working there and would walk to and from work. Doug's father was retired by then, and the yard was managed by his half-brother, but Doug and I pretty much ran the day-to-day operation. The yard had four railways for fishing vessels and ferries that needed to be hauled out for maintenance or bottom painting and repairs. Huge spools of motorized cables were used to haul and launch these boats. There was also two travel lifts for the smaller boats and also three dry sheds for boat storage and multiple floating docks for wet storage.

Doug lived at the eel farm on Fire Island and commuted five miles across the bay every day. I learned about boats, navigation, fishing, and duck hunting from Doug. If someone had a problem with anything doing with boats, the Shipyard could fix it. In those days, some of the most expensive beautiful boats were wooden. Fiberglass was just taking hold bigtime on some of the smaller-to-larger vessels, but the wooden boats needed more maintenance with repairs including caulking the bottom seams to prevent leaking, painting, and replacing any wood rot. The yard had a wood shop and a mechanical shop with specialized boat carpenters and mechanics for engine maintenance and repair to keep the boats running. Boat engine rooms are cramped and much more difficult than auto engines in terms of access to even tasks as simple as engine oil changes. It was tough, laborious work. There was one of the larger Fire Island ferry terminals in Bay Shore, which we worked on keeping them running.

I learned how to paint boats from top to bottom. Bottom painting was constant to help slow down growth from attaching to the bottoms of boats, affecting how fast a boat can travel without burning too much fuel and shortening the engine life.

Above the water line, the sides, railings, decks, trim work, and bright work finishing were all jobs that were regularly completed every day. I can tell you if you can paint a multimillion-dollar yacht and make it look new, you can be very proud.

Doug and I would also be called on to go to different marinas and docks to tow boats back to the yard for repairs. One of my favorite memories was being called on a weekend to tow a boat that had sprung a leak offshore to haul it for repairs. It was a commercial crabbing vessel, and the captain paid us to go get some beer and, while repairs were being done, threw a bushel of crabs to us to cook right at the dock—fresh ocean crabs and beer, pretty good meal!

I would tell people about some of the crazy things Doug would do that they thought I was exaggerating. I used to say he was like Tarzan! One such occurrence was being called over to guide a sport fishing boat though the Fire Island inlet that was sometimes a nightmare navigating especially in bad weather. It was blowing pretty hard, and we guided the captain to where they were going to stay at the island. When we started to get close to where they were going, the boat started to get into water that was too shallow. When we warned him, the captain slammed the boat into reverse without realizing he was towing a Boston Whaler behind the boat. Normally, this boat was stored in a cradle on the front deck of his boat. When he put it in reverse, the propeller caught the tow line and sucked the boat under the stern. We yelled for him to drop his anchor before the wind would blow him up onto the beach, and when he did, Doug put a knife between his teeth and dove overboard and cut the line loose from the prop! Out popped the whaler with a slice out of the bow as if someone had neatly cut a piece from it. Better repair that loose a multimillion-dollar yacht on the beach. The knife between his teeth is why I would tell people he was like Tarzan. I had many adventures like that when I was with Doug. Another time I remember us just offshore fishing for striped bass, and when we were heading back right along the shore break, Doug suddenly backed off on the throttle. I knew he had spotted something and started looking around and I spotted a large blue shark. Doug threw a line with one the live eels we were using for stripers, and the shark swallowed it. When he tried to set the hook, it pulled out of its mouth because it was too small a hook that we used for smaller fish. The shark swam up right next to the boat, and Doug leaned over the side with a little hand gaff and tried to grab it. I yelled, "Doug, you're crazy! It's going to pull you, me, and the gaff right overboard!" Luckily, the shark sounded when the gaff was stuck in the water. Then, a cop pulled up on the beach and started giving us a hard time about being too close to the beach. We told him there is a shark swimming about fifteen feet from swimmers in the ocean. He shut up.

Doug and I fished and hunted together with extreme success. Hunting ducks was the winter sport that local men took up. Doug had learned as a boy from his father and was a deadeye shot. The best duck hunting weather is when it's blowing, rough, and raining and especially if the snow is flying. The birds keep moving and do not light too long in that weather. You can see big flights of them way up in the sky searching for other birds in the water, and you would get their attention with decoys set up just right to bring them close to the duck boat you were lying down in. They would come flying in fast, the boat bobbing up and down in the waves, and the birds banking back and forth in flight. It was tough to knock one down. We always had Arnold with us, a mixed lab retriever that would bring the ducks we got right back to us.

We used the boatyards wood shop after hours to build a number of wooden boats called Dories. These looked similar to row boats but were sixteen feet long with high sides to make it easy to lean your knees against to stand and fish over the sides. We used oak for the ribs and rails to make them solid and marine plywood for the siding and bottoms. We fiberglassed the bottoms to prevent leaking. We put outboard engines on them and kept them at the eel farm to rent them to people vacationing on Fire Island. We would give lessons on how to operate them and make sure they were safe enough to run without hurting anyone. What a bunch of idiots they were (we called them *cityots*, "city idiots"). We would constantly have to go save and tow them back, but we made some money for a couple of seasons. We sold most of them, but I kept one, and we gave one to my father. Another time we got a call to open the yard on a weekend because a sport fishing boat was sinking offshore. When we got to the yard, there was a whole crew waiting for the boat to make it to the yard, and what happened surprised us. The boat made it in without sinking, but when we hauled it out with the travel lift, it was obvious that the fiberglass had delaminated from the bottom. Bad glass job from a new manufacturer would have pretty much ended their business if word got out. When we got it set on the trailer they brought to the yard to move the damaged boat, the crew of men shrink-wrapped it immediately with white shrink wrap so that no one could tell who the manufacturer was. They must have eventually figured out the right process because they are still building these boats today.

I enjoyed working at the shipyard, but Donna and I wanted to eventually start a family, and I just wasn't earning enough. I had to make a change. Before I found another path, a tragedy occurred at the yard. Doug's father had retired from running the yard years earlier, but his home was right on the same property as the yard. Early one morning, a northeaster kicked up, which could be pretty destructive to coastline property, and the boats at the yard were in jeopardy of being damaged. Doug Senior had been pretty ill by this time, but the years of running the yard had him up early. When he saw it was storming, he went out in the boatyard to check and make sure boats were secured enough to handle the high winds and tide.

A workboat that was designed like a miniature tugboat named the Yard Bird was used to tow and check all the floating wet storage boats around the yard. Doug Junior had gotten to the yard early, but when he checked on his dad at the house, he couldn't find him. He just assumed he kicked into his instinctive old salty mold and was out checking the yard because of the bad weather. The Yard Bird was tied to the dock, so he wasn't on that. When I got to the yard, Doug told me he couldn't find his father, so we jumped on the Yard Bird and started searching up and down the canals to see if we could locate him. Doug finally spotted him next to a number of the small classic wooden sailboats called timberlands. Apparently, Senior had attempted to secure the lines on one of these sailboats and fell overboard. We found him underwater clutching a line tied to the boat, but it was so stormy, and in his weakened condition, he didn't have the strength enough to pull himself out. Bad morning! Doug was distraught. You could live two lifetimes and not had the boating knowledge this man had.

Career and Resident Changes

I'm not sure if we moved before or after I left the shipyard, but it was time for me after growing up and living in Bay Shore to try something different. I can tell you I married a special woman who put up with many of my faults. I had a wild streak, and she helped keep me on the straight and narrow. I was still going to the local hangouts for happy hour. As long as I let Donna know where I was, she was okay with it for the most part. I started to take advantage of that. One time, I didn't tell her I was stopping, and she had made dinner. I was so late for dinner, she had it in the oven too long. When I showed up with my friend Bobby and walked in the front door, she threw the plate at me, and the baked potato was cooked so long it just bounced off the wall and across the floor, and I laughed! Bobby just spun around and beat feet. We made up, and I tried to be better about my behavior. We finally put enough money away, and with the help of her parents, Jack and Dolores, for us, along with Linda and Dennis, to buy an old Victorian-style house in Sayville. The house was big and had a big yard and a wraparound screened porch. The first floor had a large living room with a fireplace, a dining room, and a kitchen. You could access the second floor from staircases in both the front and rear of the house and with bedrooms upstairs. I started working with Dennis and our Uncle Jack at the shoe store. Linda began teaching, and Donna would become a dental assistant and travel back and forth to West Islip on the bus to her dentist's office. She said she liked riding on the bus back then.

Sayville was really nice with businesses along Main that were very popular. Dennis and I would walk to work. Selling shoes at retail was the beginning of us both learning how to become accomplished with the selling of different store stock besides shoes.

The store was primarily a children's shoe store, but we also sold men's and women's shoes. The big drawer was having a reputation for being able to fit children with the proper size shoe and also having the most well-known children shoe line manufacturer available.

Linda and Donna worked hard on decorating and fixing up the house. We were on our way to the future.

Linda and Donna's mother and father lived in Bay Shore but also had a house at Kismet on Fire Island. My brothers spent a lot of time in Kismet. I did also, plus time at Atlantique, Ocean Beach, and all along the island. Fire Island is a barrier island and runs pretty much the length of Long Island, protecting the mainland from storms, hurricanes, and flooding, approximately five miles across the Great South Bay. I spent my youth at the ocean at Fire Island at all the different little towns along the island but mostly Kismet. The house the Lyons family had at Kismet was one that their father had bought at auction on the mainland and floated it on barges across the bay and moved it to the lot where he worked hard on fixing the house up for initially a vacation home but eventually staying there full time. It was a brilliant idea he had, and it was only one of a few times it was attempted.

The Kismet Inn was a restaurant and bar at the bay side with a harbor for boat docking. In the summer, the only way to get to the island was by boat or ferry unless you were a full-time resident, you could have a permit to drive on the ocean, but all the full-time residents had four-wheel drive vehicles, and people still got stuck. Once in a while, the ocean would catch the worst drivers too.

The Kismet Inn was referred to as the Inn by locals. It was the place to go for fun, food, and drinks. After a while, someone opened another place right next to the Inn and named it The Out. Both places were always busy. Behind The Out were tennis courts, and you could always find Donna and Linda's father, Jack, playing tennis there. He was a spectacular athlete. Tennis was taken up late in his life, but he mastered the game. His family nicknamed him Ted because when he was young, he played baseball and was so good, they nicknamed him after Ted Williams, a Hall of Fame baseball player.

My brother Mike was married to Liz, whose father and brothers built many homes on Fire Island including at Kismet. I worked with one of her brothers for a bit when I was young.

I was working with Kurt, Liz's brother, at a job site in Bay Shore one day with his foreman (I can't remember his name; I think it was Jeff). He was a black fellow that was originally from down South and was really good at what he did. We were knocking down an old building to make room for a new one, and when we knocked a wall down, a possum sprung out of the wall. Jeff took off running after it as if he was Jesse Owens, grabbed it by the tail and threw it into a trash bin, slammed the lid down and turned to me, and said, "Dinner tonight!" I laughed my ass off. I did quite a bit of hunting and fishing in my life, and I eat what I catch, and in the South, that's what everyone does. Another educational experience. We also built many of what they called substations as subcontractors for the water department. These were transition water connections built underground by concrete. The site was dug out with a backhoe, and huge panels were set in to pour concrete in for the walls. That was tough work picking these panels up and pinning them together with a space between them for a truck to pour the mixture down. When the concrete finally set, we would have to peel the forms of the concrete for use for the next one. After one use, they became heavy to move. Hard labor! After the forms were peeled off the inside of the pump station, there were seams where the forms had connected together, and those seams had to be smoothed out with a concrete grinder and be finished with a special waterproof paint.

One day, I was dropping steel rebar off the back of a truck, and it caught my wedding ring and almost took my finger off. The doctor had to cut the ring off and pretty much sew my finger back on. I stopped wearing my wedding ring and any jewelry, including wristwatches, since that happened. We did all kinds of labor-intensive work, and we all worked hard and looked forward to quitting time so we could go to happy hour for a cold beer. While we are on that subject, my first job in the morning on the way to work was to go to the beer distributor and get a case of beer. Kurt would crack open one first thing in the morning and continue all day. He was a hard worker, and you wouldn't know he had had a sip until quitting time hit. It was as if a switch was thrown; at four o'clock, he was stumbling and slurring. Starting over the next day, it was the same thing. I was an eighteen-year-old kid in the best condition of my life, and I tried to keep up with him once and ended up asleep on some bags of cement mix by ten o'clock in the morning.

It was now time to change jobs. I went back to work at the shoe store with my brother and uncle for a short time until I was offered a job with a Fortune 500 company as an outside salesman. That company was a major vacuum manufacturer. No, it wasn't door-to-door sales like some companies used to do in the old days but was dealing with mom-and-pop-owned appliance store owners. I must have been pretty good at it because I started to move up the ladder. I was traveling around Long Island and ended up working out of an office in White Plains, New York, a city just northwest of Manhattan. I then ended up in the Brooklyn office until they promoted me to area sales manager in Manhattan. I commuted on the Long Island Rail Road into Penn Station and then walked across town to Park Avenue to my office on the 20th floor of the office building. My office looked out at the Empire State Building—pretty cool. As area sales manager, I supervised six different salesmen that were responsible for calling on the small appliance and camera stores throughout the city. Besides supervising them, I was also responsible for calling on the purchasing departments of the major department stores such as Macy's, Bloomingdales, Gimbels, etc. These purchasing departments were responsible for buying stock for the stores throughout the tristate area, and they had a very large budget. Another addition to my education. The salesmen respected and liked me, even though I was pretty young for that position, and I used to go with them quite often to meet their clients, all sections of the city from the South Bronx to the Lower East Side, all different cultures and types of people.

The first time I went with the salesman that handled the South Bronx (I think his name was John) to meet his clients was pretty eye-opening to me. We saw in one day a bank robbery, a motorcycle slide under an eighteen-wheeler, and a car go through a store front window. He said, "Welcome to the Bronx!" He had been born and raised there, and he was used to seeing all kinds of things. He told me he had been mugged a couple of times, but he now carried a weapon that was a telescoping stainless-steel rod that slid open if he needed to defend himself and could break an arm if he used it—totally illegal but better than being murdered.

One of my salesmen was born and raised in little Italy (his name was Tony). Everyone in little Italy knew him. He invited me to go with him when they held the Feast of San Genaro, where they would close the street for venders to cook and provide drinks. We would approach a vendor, and they would exclaim, "Tony!" So happy to see him. He introduced me to them, and we ate and drank without spending a penny. It was great fun.

My further education was meeting and dealing with the Hasidic Jews. They taught me how to negotiate, very good businessmen. They were tough negotiators, but what I learned was you could get to a point and tell them emphatically, "That's the best deal I can do," and that was it. They respected firmness. One of my salesmen was a little Jewish man named Harry. He was from Brooklyn and had taken me under his wing when I was new and was really the man who taught me how to sell professionally. He ended up selling for me commercial equipment manufactured under a separate label. There were big floor machines, vacuums, and floor wax machines, the kind you would see in big office buildings or airports, and even equipment what they called truck mount carpet cleaners. Harry's clients were big cleaning supply companies that dealt with him for years. Harry was a good and funny guy. I remember one day we were having lunch in the New York Steakhouse, and when I bit into a salad, a large carton staple was in the salad, probably popped off; when they opened the box, the lettuce came in. Harry said, "Pretend you're choking on it. We'll own this place. I know an attorney!"

I told him, "Harry, I couldn't keep a straight face!" I started laughing. They comped our meal. I'm pretty sure he was just kidding. We got along real good.

My boss was a regional manager that was originally from Chile named Fred. He and I led the country in sales percentage, and he was another one I got along with. I remember the competition with other regions that were always jealous of our success and would challenge us all the time and occasionally bet us on sales percentage for the quarter. One quarter, a manager I couldn't stand bet on us for the quarter results. I took the bet. Each month, the results would be tabulated to keep track of how everyone was doing, and for two months, we were behind. This manager kept running his mouth and rubbing it in, and I finally had enough and told him if he wanted to double the bet, I was in. He accepted. Big mistake! I knew I had a big deal brewing that I held off till the very last minute, and when the final results came in, he was shocked. He tried to welch on the bet, but I embarrassed him in front of all the other managers, and he paid up. I am not a gambler, unless it's a sure thing, and I laughed when I knew I set him up to double the bet. Lesson: Don't mess with someone whose father was a gambler. He kept his mouth shut from then on.

Fred would take me to happy hour once in a while at the end of the day before I caught a train or subway to head home. I was a beer drinker and would have a couple beers with him before I left. Fred was raised in Chile, and apparently, gin was a popular drink there, and his favorite drink was a Tanqueray martini. One afternoon, I thought I would try one, and before I knew it, I was trying to keep up with him. I lost count at six. I apparently caught a subway to Penn Station, but I ended up at a stop in Brooklyn before I realized it. I had to get off and go over to the opposite platform to catch the subway back into Penn. I finally got the train to Long Island. The ride if the trains were on time was typically an hour and a half, but the trains were always late. By the time it arrived at my station, it was the middle of the night, and as I walked into the station's building, I threw up all over. I can't stand to even smell gin to this day.

I knew they were grooming me for bigger things. I was young and aggressive, and I think I was street-smart. There is a difference between being book-smart and being street-smart. Street-smart can keep you safer in a big city if you know how to act. Really, sales is very similar to acting, and I was pretty good at it. Being around cops and detectives my whole life gave me insight on how to act like I was a cop. If I was walking down a street or side street past some unsavory-looking person or people (punks), I wore a suit for work, and I looked like a detective would look, and I would tap my jacket like I was packing and checking to make sure my weapon was under my arm. It seemed to work because they would avoid eye contact or coming too close to me. Once in a while, I would have to be in the office early to conduct a sales meeting, and I would drive in. I would park in a lot on the East Side, and one day, I drove just past the entrance by mistake and turned into a driveway to back up and get back to the entrance. I stopped the car to get back, and while waiting for some traffic to pass since it wasn't quite light yet, a hooker reached into the window between my legs and asked if I wanted a date. In shock I said, "No, I have to go work."

She exclaimed, "Faggot!" And then she walked away. I made sure I didn't ever miss that parking entrance again.

The city that never sleeps—I commuted into the city for seven years, and at the time, I loved New York. The city was rough. It was when Koch was mayor, and it was dirty and crime-ridden, with all kinds of garbage strikes, and it was dangerous too, but I knew how to handle myself. If I had some free time, I would go to a museum or to the New York Library. I learned how to get around and see most of the city. That changed when something happened at work. The big management came to me and told me Harry had to open new accounts and if he didn't, I would have to fire him. I tried to explain how Harry worked. He had loyal customers who loved him. To give you an example, if my quarterly numbers were soft, I would tell Harry, and he would call one of his clients, and the conversation would go something like this: "Hey, Joe, I'm gonna send you a dozen of this a dozen of that."

They always responded, "Okay, Harry, whatever you want." He had that close a relationship with them, and he never lacked or missed his numbers. They said they didn't care; he had to open new accounts.

I told them, "Fuck you! If you want to fire him, you fire him, but I'm not!"

That was the beginning of the end. They demoted Harry to what they call a demonstrator, the one you used to see in appliance sections of department stores throwing dirt on the carpet and demonstrating how well the vacuum picked the dirt up. I didn't want to see Harry lose his benefits, so I went along with it. He did that for two weeks, had a heart attack, and died. I was heartbroken.

I didn't want my life to end up like that. Donna and I had gone on a vacation with friends to Hilton Head Island before this happened. I really loved it, and so did Donna. I asked her if she wanted to move there, and she said yes.

I told the company to shove it since I realized all a person is in a corporation is a number, not a human being, and I didn't want to end up a number and let them have that control over me and do to me what they did to Harry.

We put a plan together and disgusted our plan with Dennis and Linda.

It was going to be hard to leave since we had so much fun living in that house together. We used to have great parties there with family and friends. We had children while living there. Donna and I had Donald Junior and Andrew, and Linda and Dennis had Deirdre and Evan. Christmas parties were a hoot. We would rotate between Mike and Liz's house and our house. The brothers would take turns playing Santa, and that alone would result in the hardest laughter you ever heard. We worked out a plan to sell half of the house to Linda and Dennis. Donna's parents by this time had actually bought a villa on Hilton Head Island, so we did have a place to stay until we worked out a place of our own.

Hilton Head Island Adventure

We packed up our old station wagon with as much as we could including our children and headed South, a ballsy move that my wife supported not knowing what was in store for us. Neither of us had jobs, but I thought I would find something to make a living. It was tough at first, but we came up with a plan for that also. I started to offer first repainting villas and then existing houses and eventually hooked up with a builder to paint new homes. If you can paint multimillion-dollar yachts, painting a house was easy. Our plan was for me to work during the day, and Donna found a job waiting on tables at a local rib joint at night so I could watch the kids at night. It worked out for a while. Donna likes to say she wasn't very good at waitressing, but she really was but would always tell people it was her first night so they would feel okay with her service and taking orders, and most people tipped more, feeling sorry for her. I was doing pretty good initially with painting even to the point where I hired some help. I had hooked up with one of the most popular decorating firms on Hilton Head, and he gave me the contract to repaint Harbor Town golf clubhouse. That was pretty cool—painting the exterior trim and benches even the distinctive striped canvas awnings grey. That's when I started to get tickets to the PGA event, The Heritage Golf Tournament, held there every year right after the Masters was played in Augusta just a week before. It was pretty cool having full access passes to the clubhouse, even the locker room where I would see the top players of that era.

Eventually, what happened is the cheaper labor showed up. They started doing jobs cheaper, and because they had multiple people on a crew, they completed jobs faster. I had to admit they were very efficient, and they really didn't have as much overhead because they would house ten people in a small resident. That pretty much put me out of business, so I had to find something else. Another time to struggle.

My sons were very young. Donald was preschool age, and Andrew was just a toddler. We were only on Hilton Head Island a few months when Andrew started complaining that his leg hurts. He had a fever and was not showing signs of getting better, and we ended up taking him to the emergency room at Hilton Head Hospital. One of our neighbors offered to watch Donald while we went to the hospital. When they examined him, they found that he had appendicitis and that it had ruptured. He was in pretty bad shape, and the doctors told us they weren't really equipped to handle his illness properly and suggested he be transferred to MUSC Children's Hospital in Charleston about an hour ride from Hilton Head. They let Donna ride in the ambulance with him but would not allow us both. One of the nurses told me she had trained at MUSC and said she could direct me to the emergency room. By now, it was totally dark out, and I had no idea where I was going. I had this beat-up old station wagon and filled it with fuel, checked the oil and water, and took off following the nurses' directions. I entered the ER and asked where my son was, and they said he wasn't there yet. I sped so fast I beat the ambulance. When they got there and the doctors examined him, they came out to explain what the plan was. The doctor that was explaining to us appeared to me to be no older than a teenager, and it freaked me out so much, I told him, "You're not operating on my son. I want someone more experienced."

They realized how upset I was, and the head of the department, the man who taught the interns, came in and assured me *he* would operate. That surprised the staff, but that man saved my son's life in my view. I found out later that MUSC is a top teaching school, and any of the doctors would have been more than capable of performing the operation. Donna stayed with Andrew in his room during his recovery, and I stayed at the Ronald McDonald House, right next door to the hospital. The charity staff was wonderful, caring for families who had children much sicker than our child. Welcome to the South.

Donna found a job at a property management company, and I started to look for something in sales I knew I could do. I finally found a job selling water treatment systems for a local company that had a known name brand. They had systems that treated water hardness, odor, and purity, and with the large boom of new homes going on in the Hilton Head Island and surrounding areas, there was a great demand for them. While I was selling, Donna was working for a property management company in a resort community named Palmetto Dunes. Palmetto Dunes is an oceanfront plantation on Hilton Head Island known for its beautiful access to the ocean and three different golf courses. Our boys were in school by now, so we would work our schedule around theirs. We had decided to move to Hilton Head because we had vacationed with some friends who had relatives who owned property there and invited us to visit. I played golf with Gerry during the day, and Donna explored the island with Jeannie, and then we would meet up for dinner somewhere. We decided we really liked Hilton Head Island. It was sometimes chaotic, and there were times I struggled to make ends meet, but both of us decided we wouldn't give up and continue to try and make it work.

The best decision we ever made was getting out of New York. I am even more convinced of that now that I see what has happened to that State recently. What has happened to the city itself is heartbreaking. A city I used to love I don't think will ever recover from the woke politics that have infected a city that used to be beautiful.

During the summer months, when we were working, the kids attended a summer program for children called Kindred Spirits. One year, our nephew Darrin came down and stayed with us and helped us out watching the kids.

Darrin would sometimes go out and stay out after his curfew. That worried me because we had promised his mother we would keep an eye on him. One night, he didn't come home. I freaked out calling the hospitals, going around the island, and checking all the bars, restaurants, etc. We finally got a call from him.

"Darrin where the hell are you?"

He said, "Hold on for a minute." He had to look at the phone he was calling from, and it said The Westen, an oceanfront hotel! He had apparently hooked up with someone staying there. I told him to stay where he was, and I went and got him. I never squealed on him or told his parents till now. Darrin and I became very close, and we would go out together from time to time. I figured it was best if I stayed around him as much as possible to keep him out of trouble. We would usually go to places that had live music. One of our favorite places was the OPO (old post office). It was the original post office on Hilton Head that was turned into a music club. There was good music all the time. Our favorite was a reggae band called "Ital."

One day, he was watching the kids for us, and when Donna and I came home, there was a bunch of Beaufort County Sherriff officers swarming around the villa complex near our villa, scaring the shit out of us. They all had their guns drawn like they were going after a mass murderer (running around like what I called the keystone cops), but it was a woman who lived next door that was a teacher. She was a drunk and had a fight with her sister and shot and killed her and then tried to commit suicide, shooting herself in the head. Darrin was smart enough to hide the kids, and he came out on our landing and gave us the thumbs up to let us know the kids were fine. When the cleaning crew came in to finally clean up this villa, the empty bottles and cans almost reached the ceiling.

Hilton Head was really just starting to grow and was only a tourist destination during "the season" and was a great place to raise our kids. Now, it's a yearlong destination for what we call Tourons (tourist morons). The problem I found is they begin to think they are the only important people on the planet, acting as if they were better than anyone else. It was as if they filed their brains as soon as they crossed into South Carolina. Maybe it's only my response to stupid people. The spring did become a spring break destination for idiot college kids who crowded the beaches, trashing them with empty beer cans and loud music—a few idiots ruining it for the locals who were used to smaller crowds and beautiful beaches. I used to like to sit on the beach with the family and a cooler and have a beer. We always have and always will clean up after ourselves because we respect other people and the environment. It wasn't long before they made it illegal to drink on the beach and for a few *Tourons* to ruin it for it for the rest of us. It is still a beautiful beach with calm ocean waves.

Donna and I eventually bought a villa in a gated community called Shipyard Plantation. Family and friends came to visit us on a regular basis. My brother Mike and his wife, Liz, bought a villa near us for vacationing when they had time off and rented it short term when not here, so we were able to see them once in a while. My boys started school in the local schools and spent their spare time skateboarding and learning how to surf.

I wasn't a surfer but had spent my whole life with surfers and body surfing and splashing around the ocean, and I began to teach my boys how to surf in the calm ocean by sitting them on the board and pushing them toward the beach when a wave was big enough. They eventually were able to stand. They got better and better at it. Back in New York, John (my brother-in-law) was one of the best surfers I knew as good as or the same as Doug Brewster. I watched them surf, and a crowd would form to watch how good they were. Watching them surf was a lesson all on its own on how to and used the knowledge of them catching waves to help me teach the boys.

The boys got better and better because they attended a daycare center together (Kindred Spirits) run by Hamp Sewell, an old soul surfer who also ran a surf school on Hilton Head. Hamp's son Byron was a surfer around the same age as my sons, and they surfed together on Hilton Head. The surf did get pretty good if a storm was swinging by, and Byron got to be so good that even though he learned on small waves, he became the East Coast Junior Surf Champion. He is also a nice guy that is still friends with my sons to this day.

Growing up on Hilton Head Island was setting up the boys experiences to be pretty special. They both were good athletes. Besides surfing, they skateboarded with the other kids and hung out at the local surf and skateboard shop with the owner of the shop's son. They all built a ramp to jump, and when they weren't surfing, they were skating and kept active all the time. They also played sports, baseball, football, and basketball, and were pretty good at all. I coached both boys in youth baseball, a league similar to Little League, but in the South, they called it Dixie Youth Baseball. Andrew was a great catcher and hitter, and so was Donald, who was also a middle fielder at second base. I enjoyed coaching, but Donna wasn't really fond of watching the boys play. I think she found it a little too stressful. Donald also played youth football as a quarterback. He had a great arm. Putting the baseball teams together was about choosing players from a tryout of kids who wanted to play and selections of them rotated team by team. I had a knack of watching kids who never played and seeing their potential, not by watching them swing, run, or throw but just watching how they walked across the field. There is something about the way an athlete moves. You could tell they had potential and that good coaching would make them players. I was usually right.

We rarely lost a game with the kids that played for us, again it being a team sport with good players. I coached with another coach who had played college baseball at UNC. We were a good pair and never put pressure on any of the kids, just telling them to try hard and have fun, and they did. We did practice a lot, but the kids loved it. Andrew played also, and there were times when I helped coach both of the boys games the same day. Donald was older than Andrew and played in a different age group.

Rob would pitch batting practice after I ran out of steam, but he seemed to not ever get tired. I was selected as an assistant coach for the Dixie Youth state team, and along with Rob after winning the local championship, we went to the state championship. We were the first coaches to take a Hilton Head Island team to the States. This was pretty special since the selection of players on the island was limited because the year-round population was small at that time. Donald was selected to be on the team. Around the time of the state tournament, my father was pretty ill. He had gotten a chance to visit us on the island before he was sick, but it had been a while.

I had to fly to New York because my dad passed and the games had started, so I missed a couple of games. When I arrived back, we had another game after having won a couple of games. Donald hit a homerun over the fence, and when he made it back to the dugout, he told me, "That was for Grandpa."

We ultimately got beat, but it was really special. The boys continued to play sports through high school.

Donna had changed jobs and was now working at an oceanfront hotel in Palmetto Dunes Plantation. I changed jobs also and went to work for an HVAC, plumbing, and electric private South Carolina-owned company.

Where Donna worked, they had three golf courses, and I played some golf when I had time. Andrew took an interest in golf and was hanging at the course quite a lot. He would help out as a kid doing little odd jobs around the course and also began to play. He began to become a good player and continued to play into high school, playing on the high school golf team. He also played baseball in high school. Andrew asked me to take him to Palmetto Dunes to watch an NCAA golf final because he told me he wanted to see a player. I didn't know who it was at the time, but it turned out to be Tiger Woods! When I saw him tee off, I had never seen anybody hit the ball like that, and I was shocked to say the least. I have a picture some place of Andrew lying down alongside a green watching him putt. You could walk alongside the players as they played, and it was a time that I didn't realize how lucky we were to see that. Tiger lost in a playoff to a player who drained a very long putt. That was the last time he came to Hilton Head Island to play.

Andrew continued to hang out on the golf course and play golf. He played for his high school golf and basketball team. At that time in his young life, he was really good at golf and still liked playing and asked the teaching pros about possibility of becoming a teaching pro, but all the pros told him that teaching takes up so much of your time that they really didn't get much time to actually play and suggested for him if he liked golf to maybe find something else in the industry to do. He decided he would get into golf course maintenance and put a plan together to follow that plan. His brother Donald decided to get into the food service industry, and when he graduated high school, he applied to culinary school at Trident Culinary in Myrtle Beach. When he graduated, he became a full-blown chef and started his career in local restaurants. I was so impressed with his talent. When he came home, he would cook for us occasionally and could put a delicious meal together even when we had what we thought was not much in our pantry or refrigerator to do so. He had a talent and knack for great meals.

Andrew graduated and attended Horry Georgetown for agronomy and started a career as an assistant superintendent at a local course after he attained his degree. He stayed in the industry for a while and eventually ended up as head superintendent at a different course where he met his future wife, Jennifer (J-Bug).

I have a few funny golf stories about me playing golf with my friends but also one story I won't ever forget about when Andrew (Drew) invited me to play golf at the course he was an assistant. This course was a member's-only course, very exclusive with memberships very much like the membership at Augusta is exclusive. Some of the members were so wealthy, they would fly in their private planes into an airport very close to the course, play a round, and fly out. I was very honored for Drew to invite me, especially since my game wasn't very good, rarely breaking 100. What did help my game was you had to have a caddy with you.

We had played a few holes and had hit the ball down the fairway when Drew saw a couple of the maintenance men; he called to them, and when we got up to them, Drew started speaking to them in fluent Spanish. I had no idea he could speak Spanish and was shocked I didn't know he could. I turned to him and said, "When the fuck did you learn to speak Spanish?" He told me if he couldn't speak Spanish, it would be hard for him to communicate what he needed to get done. That really came as a surprise to me and made me proud of how much smarter he was than I was.

I wasn't a very good golfer. It was to me really just a reason to hang out with friends and drink beer. We had a tight group of friends and would play different courses around the Hilton Head area.

One funny story was playing and hitting the ball down the middle of a fairway and was a little more than 150 yards from the green. Some courses would use white PVC sticking up to mark the 150-mark distance to the green, and I used it as a target toward the green. When I hit the ball, it smashed into the PVC, and it exploded as if someone had put a firecracker in it and scattered it around the fairway. I pulled out what was left and turned it upside down and stuck it back in the ground. Another round I was with friends and playing better than I normally did and was feeling a little cocky. I had a short distance to the green on one hole, but I used the wrong club, thinking I was using a shorter club, and although I hit the ball right toward the flag, it rolled off the back of the green into a little drainage ditch behind the green. I pulled my cart around to the ball, and by this time, my friends were all on the green waiting for me. Feeling cocky, I announced, "Watch this," and when I hit the ball, I shanked it, and it hit a little wooden bridge, and the ball bounced back and hit me right on the end of my penis. *Oof!* I bent over in pain and looked up at the green, and everyone was lying on the green, laughing their asses off. It took me three holes to pull my penis out of my stomach!

I used to play more golf with my good friend Johnny. I stopped playing, but Johnny still plays. I used to go to happy hour once in a while with friends, and Donna was okay with that as long as I let her know before I did. One time, I neglected to tell her and came home late. She was apparently furious as she didn't know where I was because, when I came home and rushed to the bathroom, I noticed, as I walked past the closet, my portion was empty. I looked out the window, and my clothes, golf clubs, and all other things were strewn out the back in the rain. I never forgot to tell her where I was again after that experience. She eventually forgave me. Thank God!

Another Job Change

I mentioned I changed jobs earlier. Water treatment just became where it wasn't lucrative enough especially since I thought the owner wasn't inventive enough to grow fast enough for me to make a good living. I sometimes struggled but tried to be optimistic about getting through the hard times, seeing light at the end of the tunnel. Donna pulled through again and took the job in conference services at an oceanfront hotel. I was offered a job for a company that contracted plumbing, electric, and HVAC services. This was a privately owned company operating in the state of South Carolina that opened a branch in the Hilton Head area. They wanted me for outside sales, selling replacement equipment to existing homes with aging or broken heat and air systems. I attended training from manufacturers like Carrier and Trane to understand the workings and differences of how these machines operate. More education, but I felt once I learned about the equipment, I had so much sales experience over the course of my life, I could have taught a sales class. That's not bragging; that's a fact. I worked there for a few years before some more changes were made. A corporation purchased this private company and started to expand around the country. The way they did this was by buying smaller private electrical, plumbing, and HVAC companies in the locations they wanted to expand. That's how I met my future boss. This company purchased a local company named Dean Heating and Air from Charles Dean Sr. They absorbed the workforce from Deans including his sons, Charlie and Paul. The smart thing Charles did to protect his name was only signing a two-year working contract with them. It wasn't long before Charlie and Paul realized corporate life wasn't for them, having grown up in a family-run business and not being just another number on a corporate ledger. They were done dealing with red tape and corporate rules that they seemed to change every day and decided after the contract ran out that they were done. I saw the handwriting on the wall after my experience in the corporate world. He asked me if I wanted to go, and I said yes. I watched as the corporate heads escorted him out of the building as if he was some sort of criminal. He told me to hold on until he put his plan together and he would let me know when to come.

He finally called me, and off I went. His family owned a large property complex that had originally been used for testing of monkeys to help find a vaccine for polio. They called it the monkey farm, and when Salk discovered the vaccine, they just packed up and sold the property to Charles Senior. His home was built on the property along with Paul's and Charlie's. When he started the business back up, the warehouses used for testing needed to be remodeled, so we set up shop in Charlie's garage until remodeling was complete enough to use as offices and warehousing. It was slow beginnings, and I did struggle to make ends meet but again was optimistic about seeing light at the end of the tunnel.

We started to grow the business with help from a number of good people who came over with us from the previous corporation we all left. Charlie's wife, Anne, covered the phone and scheduling. They all knew I was from New York, and one day, Anne came back from her house and told me "Don, someone just flew a plane into the World Trade Center." I asked her if it looked like it was foggy there. She said no, so we went back to her house to watch what was going on. I couldn't believe it when we saw the second plane hit the second tower. I knew we were under attack. Everybody knows where they were when that occurred. Donna called me and told me that she had clients that had plans to come to the hotel where she was working as the director of conference services and that they tried to contact them but the number they tried just stayed busy. They later found that almost the entire company was lost in the attack.

I had spent time in the towers while working in New York, and we had also attended school with a set of twins that worked there. One brother had been at the tower when they had attempted a bombing earlier in the parking garage. When the first plane hit, he called his brother in the other tower and told him to get out, and they both survived. A friend of mine on Hilton Head, Ronzo, married to C Roll, told me about her brother who was an EMT in New York and made it to the site and was taking photos on the way, which ended up in I think *Time* magazine. They made it to the towers before they came down but pulled under the walkover when the buildings came down. They hid under the vehicle when it came down and survived. As Americans, we need to *never forget* what these bastards did and always remain vigilant about taking out these terrorist bastards.

The Tunnel to Towers Foundation should be donated to every American to remember the bravery of those who tried to save lives.

The Dean family was like an extension of my family, and they treated me like that. I continued to work with them, and each year got better and better as we grew the business. I made some lifelong friends working at Deans—Kylie, Joe, Klug, Grubs, Bobby, Kenny (K-Rod), and also Bob (Bo-burger) just to name a few. The one very close friend I made was Mary (Mares-E-Dotes), whom I met when she was a manufacturer representative selling equipment to the company. Mary left that company and for a short time worked alongside me selling replacement systems. She was offered a job with another manufacturer and did that for some time but got tired of all the traveling and made a decision to come back and work for Deans after I told her I was planning to retire and she could spend more time at home, not traveling away from her family as much. She did replace me, and we are very good friends. I feel that Mary is filling the void of the sister I lost, and we really get along. I feel I can talk about things with her and her with me, and we understand each other. She has a great family also.

I did have another close friend, Johnny Moralez (More-Or Less), whom I met when he was the chief engineer at the hotel Donna worked at. Johnny also worked with me running the service department at Deans but went back to hotel engineering, the job he really liked. Johnny was a tough guy, built like one with a shaved head. Johnny was raised in Bedford–Stuyvesant, a rough neighborhood in Brooklyn, New York, and he told me everyone he grew up with is either dead or in jail. That didn't stop him from success and being the smartest friend I have. He passed his intelligent gene onto three kids, who all received academic scholarships to Clemson University.

I had the opportunity to attend the Masters golf tournament a couple times, but the best was the par three they hold every year as a warm-up before the actual tournament begins. I attended the one where Palmer, Nicholas, and Woods played in the same group! We were right behind the clubhouse when they all hit up on the raised green. There is a hill that slopes down from the clubhouse to where the patrons could stand, and we watched a guy come down the hill carrying a tray full of beers for his friends. The grass was slick from a little rain, and he lost his footing and slid down the hill spilling the beer all over himself. The entire crowd cheered. It was very funny to us. What an honor to see three of the best golfers to ever play golf playing in the same group.

My son Drew left the golf industry and began a charter fishing business. He had gotten a real taste for fishing when he went down to South Florida and fished with his cousin, my godson Doug Junior, who was into commercial fishing.

Drew learned to fish by trial and error and became a top-notch fly fisherman. He hasn't picked up a golf club since and has no desire to. He built up a good business catering to fly-fishing clients. He really became good at this but got tired of dealing with people and decided to go strictly commercial fishing. I have to say, and not only because he is my son but because I have been around fishing and fishermen my whole life, he's the best fisherman I have ever seen. If you ask the charter fishing fleet around Hilton Head, they will tell you how good he is, and he has passed a lot of his prior knowledge onto some of the more successful ones and remains close to a couple of them.

He would normally go forty to fifty miles offshore alone to fish for a couple to three nights and would contact us when he came close enough to shore to get a cell phone signal to let us know he was on the way in to prevent us from being too concerned for his safety because the ocean can be dangerous and weather can change rapidly. He did sometimes use a mate from time to time but would rather fish by himself rather than have to worry about another person on the boat.

He is still fishing. Oh, by the way, his wife, J-Bug, is an ER nurse and also an excellent fly fisherman, and they sometimes plan their vacations to areas where they can fish when she is not saving lives at the ER as a nurse.

Drew battles with the red tape regulations that are antiquated and do not take into account the individual commercial fishermen and make the regulations to protect the big corporate companies that spend buckets of money lobbying and preventing the small businesses that built this country from prospering. Add the huge increases in fuel costs; because of these, uninformed climate change idiots stopping the USA from becoming energy independent again by stopping oil companies from accessing the abundance of natural resources of this country. I am hoping and praying the rest of our country wakes up to the ridiculous restrictions and brings our country back to being the world power we had always been.

Loss of Loved Ones

Being the youngest boy out of eight siblings, as I grew older, I had to prepare myself for the loss of people closest to me, including my parents. Doris was the first to go after a brave fight against breast cancer. She was a battler just like the rest of the Mahoney family is. When she had gotten sick, Donna and I were expecting our first son, Donald Junior. I asked her to fight long enough to be able to see him born, and she did manage to see him, but we lost her just before our second son, Andrew, was born. I will never forget the response of the community and friends and family when she passed.

My older brothers—Mike, Patrick, and Brian—arranged a motorcade of police motorcycles and police cars to escort her funeral procession from the services to her resting place. The escort actually shut down the Long Island Expressway for the procession, and the motorcycles would block intersections of the different crossings as we passed them. That was only one of three times I had seen that happened.

The other times were when years later when we lost Jackson PDQ. And then we lost Mike to a battle that he fought bravely to battle, a cancerous brain tumor.

When we lost Mike, we were living in Hilton Head and had to travel back to Long Island for the services.

Mike was truly the heart of our family, and I miss him every day, especially his sense of humor. I know he would laugh his ass off at his service, which was attended by all sorts of dignitaries and police officers, including the chief of police. He was in the middle of speaking about Mike's record when one of the family friends, Joe, who had been drinking heavily, interrupted and started talking, saying, "I just want to say something."

Terry, realizing it was not going to go well, sprung from his seat and grabbed Joe and rushed him outside. After the proceeding, I saw Joe's brother, Eddie, whom I played football with. Eddie was another friend of mine who was very funny, and when I asked him where Joe was, he responded, "He's probably outside working on his speech!" Eddie made me laugh. Laughter is the best medicine.

Years later, we lost my sister, Regina. Gina and I remained close our whole life. By the time she became sick with battling the same disease as Doris, she was living in South Florida with Phil. She lived fairly close to where her son, Doug Junior, was living, married with two children, a granddaughter and grandson.

I mentioned my niece Kerri and how we are very close. One reason is Kerri and Gina were close and Kerri would make a real effort to keep in touch with Gina during her illness. Kerri has this great laugh and the Mahoney sense of humor, and Gina would brighten up and laugh every time they spoke. I feel a close relationship with Kerri because of how she treated my sister. Oh and she was born on St. Patrick's Day and is one of the few family birthdays I can remember without Donna telling me whose birthday it is. Kerri has a son, Cameron, who provided her with a grandson, Charley. We look forward to him growing up and watching him with Shannon's daughter, Amelia.

We are very close to Evan and Deirdre, my nephew and niece, Dennis and Linda's children, for obvious reasons. They are as close as being our own children without actually being our children because of the close bloodlines of brothers being married to sisters. I joke with Kerri that she's my favorite niece, next to Deirdre.

Phil and Gina had a daughter, Shannon, by this time, who had gotten married to Wes, and they had a daughter, Amelia. Gina had gotten some time to spend with Amelia before she got really sick, but she was as tough again as any of us and, with the help from Phil, battled hard to fight the fight. Phil was relentless, doing his own research and finding doctors who helped him keep her alive. I will always remember how hard Phil battled, and it was easy to see he really loved my sister. Phil liked to play golf and would play golf occasionally with Gina's first husband, Doug.

They had no hard feelings. Doug had moved on and would still travel back and forth from Fire Island to his home in South Florida. After we lost Gina, Dennis and I would travel down to see Phil. Phil was another one of the good guys, and he struggled with the loss of his wife and had bought a boat to live on. We had a couple of good visits with Phil. He finally years later found a friend who lived in Texas and had decided to visit her, and I think the plan was to bring her back to Florida to live on the boat with him. On the way back to Florida, Phil wasn't feeling well and decided to stop at a hotel to rest and apparently, when he walked into the lobby, had a heart attack and passed. Another one of the good guys was gone.

So it's been a little tough dealing with losing those people whom we were close to, but that is one of the reasons I am writing this.

I have to admit it is very cleansing for me.

I am hoping that some changes happen in terms of the way our country is headed for the sake of our families, children, and their children. We need to stop these liberal, communist, socialist assholes from ruining the free, beautiful country of the USA by getting rid of the *dumbacraps* in the White House and put in leaders who have the best interest of all the people for the people.

I have to close by saying my life has been an interesting adventure, and I was lucky to find the woman I still love and that I was also lucky to be born the Seventh Son of an Irishman.

Baseball Teams Make Money You Know; Mahoneys Greet 7th Son

Southside Hospital officials are checking records to see if this one can be topped anywhere in Suffolk County and in this day and age of small families it is highly unlikely. A simple birth announcement would appear such as: May 9, Mr. and Mrs. John Mahoney, Bay Shore, a boy.

With the number of births setting new records virtually every quarter-year period at the hospital, it is hard to imagine that such a simple announcement could create any kind of furor. However, there's a story behind the latest addition to the John Vincent Mahoney family, residence 122 South Clinton ave., Bay Shore:

The boy, Donald Joseph, weight eight pounds, two ounces, is the seventh child born to the Mahoneys. He is also the seventh son!

Mrs. Mahoney is the former Doris

Courtney, daughter of Mr. and Mrs. Al Courtney of 5 Atlantic st., Bay Shore. Doris was the first girl in two generations born to the Courtney family. She has five brothers. Her mother, Cecelia, was the only girl in the Kletchka family! On the paternal side, there are five Mahoney girls and three Mahoney boys.

Little Donald enters a strictly masculine atmosphere broken only by the charming femininity of his mother. His six predecessors, all delivered at the Southside Hospital and all by the same doctor, are John V. (Jay), jr., age 10; Patrick, 9; Michael, 8; Terence, 7; Brian, 5; and Dennis, 18 months.

The Courtney boys Mrs. Mahoney's brothers that is, all were very athletic. One of her brothers, Kenneth, generally is recognized as one of the top club basketball players in this area. William, John, Vincent and Donald were members of basketball and baseball teams at Bay Shore High School several years back. When the number of male offspring of the Mahoney family reached five five years ago there was talk of a family basketball team. When Dennis arrived 18 month ago the Mahoneys became expansive and talked about a hockey team.

Now, with the number at seven

there's no telling what kind of a team will be formed.

Father Jack, an employee of the General Outdoor Advertising Company's Long Island branch, was not available for comment. Mrs. Mahoney indicated, however, that basketball teams need substitutes and two subs should be sufficient. "But suppose the boys like football!", she exclaimed. "There are eleven men on a football team!"

Brian "Mooncat"

Terry the "Terrible Termite" and Dennis the "Menace"

DON MAHONEY

Mike "Moose"

Patrick "Fatrack" with baby Deefer at Benjis Beach

From left to right back row: Patrick, Dennis on Dorothy babysitters lap, Terry, Dorris holding Deefer, front row: Mike, Brian, Jay

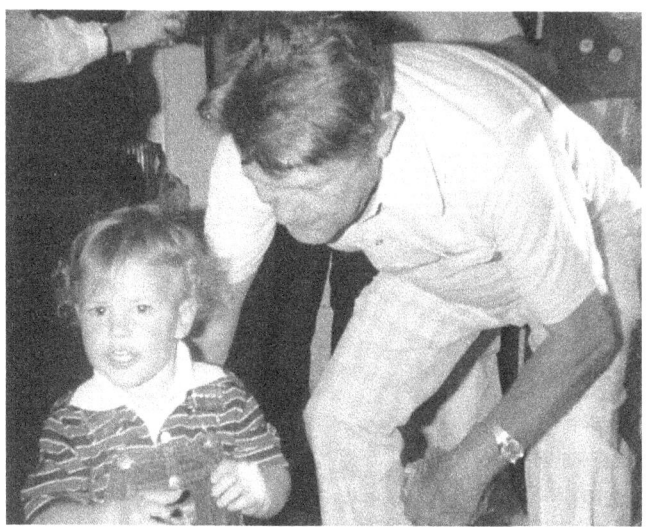

Jackson "PDQ" with Donald Jr.

Dennis and Donald early training

Jackson "PDQ" arm on rail fishing with buddies

Andrew, Deefer, Donald Jr. Fishing on my 60th birthday

Back row: Maureen, Patrick (Fatrack), Brian (Mooncat), Mike (Moose), Jay (Jayson), Donna, Doris (Mom), Jack (Dad, PDQ) Front row Gina (Bina), Don (Deefer), Dennis (The Menace) Jay and Donna's wedding

Wife, Donna speeding through Mackays Creek

About the Author

Don Mahoney lives on Hilton Head Island and is enjoying his retirement. He was born and raised streetwise in New York and is living in South Carolina for forty years. Now he claims he's "southern by the grace of God," enjoying his retirement on Hilton Head Island.

Printed in the USA
CPSIA information can be obtained
at www.ICGtesting.com
LVHW090013301024
795097LV00003B/375